BRITISH FORCES IN THE KOREAN WAR

The Korean War Memorial in St. Paul's Cathedral unveiled by Her Majesty Queen Elizabeth II on 11th March 1987.

BRITISH FORCES IN THE KOREAN WAR

Edited by

Ashley Cunningham-Boothe and Peter Farrar

Korean contact

SIR — The British Korean Veterans Association is trying to contact those people who served with HM Armed Forces in Korea or Japan during the Korean War 1950-53, and also those people who served at a later date with the Peace Keeping Forces.

James R. Grundy
4, Lightoaks Road,
Salford, M6 8NQ.
Greater Manchester.

Published by

The British Korean Veterans Association

ISBN 0 9512622 0 3

First published 1988

Published by The British Korean Veterans Association.

Printed by Reuben Holroyd Ltd.,
Hook House, Haley Hill, Halifax, West Yorkshire, HX3 6EE.

Orders, with payment to B.K.V.A., must be sent to T. A. Cunningham-Boothe, 32 Hatherell Road, Radford Semele, Leamington Spa, CV31 1UE, United Kingdom.

FOREWORD

by Major-General P. A. Downward, CB, DSO, DFC,
President, British Korean Veterans Association.

To those who served in the British forces in the Korean War, Korea was a far flung country. To the young generation of today, the phrase "far flung" may sound somewhat dramatic in this age of high-speed air travel and modern communication. But in those days it was a five week journey by troopship from England; and Korea, besides being a long way from home, was a country very strange to all of us. Not only were the terrain and climate unusual, but the United Nations force itself, to which we belonged, was an astonishing improvisation with its wide variety of fighting and logistic units, to say nothing of the many languages spoken. But out of all this, by dint of the suffering and hardship inflicted on the individual soldier, sailor and airman, as well as many joyful moments, has emerged a bond of comradeship amongst the survivors, as indeed has been seen in most other wars. Based on this comradeship has developed a strong association of men and women, known as the British Korean Veterans Association, which is also a member of the International Federation of Korean War Veterans Associations, incorporating twenty countries in all who took part in the conflict.

If anyone ever had doubts as to why he was in Korea, and what he was fighting for in the early fifties, I can only recommend that he should see Korea today with its beautiful countryside, modern cities, a thriving economy and its warm-hearted people ever appreciative of what the United Nations did for them in their hour of need. Regrettably, the struggle between the ideologies of North and South Korea that precipitated the war still goes on, and the people of the Republic of Korea must ever remain prepared and alert to the possibility of further conflict with its neighbour to the north of the 38th parallel.

We shall always remember those who did not return from Korea, and whether or not you took part in the war, I hope you will occasionally stop and think of those, who through the demands of their service in Korea, are now in need of help through the British Korean Veterans Association. The aim of this book is to raise funds for that Association; I hope you enjoy reading it.

CONTENTS

APPENDICES

LIST OF MAPS

INTRODUCTION

This book was made possible by the British Korean Veterans Association, established in 1981 from the amalgamation of two recently formed associations. Its objects are to foster the comradeship of those who served in the Korean War, to look after the welfare of members, widows and dependents and to contribute to the historical record of the war. Although many members have belonged to regimental or other associations since the war, there had not previously been a common association for all who fought in the three services and in the auxiliary nursing and welfare units. It has been remarkable how, after thirty and more years, men have resumed old friendships or formed new ones with comrades of that war.

B.K.V.A. has now about forty-five branches, spread throughout Britain. The first President was Major-General T. Brodie, CB, CBE, DSO, who commanded 29 Independent Brigade in Korea, and was succeeded in office by Major-General P. A. Downward, CB, DSO, DFC, who commanded 1913 Light Liaison Flight. The association runs a wide variety of social activities and cultivates friendly relations with Koreans, through re-visits and other contacts. A bi-annual magazine, *The Morning Calm*, is published. One of the association's proudest achievements was to secure the unveiling of the Korean War Memorial in the crypt of St. Paul's Cathedral in London on 11th March 1987 by Her Majesty the Queen.

The book is not intended to be a detailed history of every phase of military and naval contribution to the Korean War. Rather it is to give, in the opening chapter a general view, and then to illustrate some important aspects of the war by contributions from persons all of whom write from personal experience. The work of British women, small in numbers, has been high-lighted. Photographs have been selected entirely from the personal albums and collections of members and are aimed to illustrate the widest spectrum of life in and behind the front line and on the sea.

As a great amount of material was submitted, the editors had the difficult task of making selections and, in some cases, shaping it for publication. It is hoped that the result will serve to give a general knowledge of Britain's part in the war and a good impression of what it was like to be there.

PART I

ASPECTS OF THE WAR

Chapter 1

WHAT WE ACHIEVED AND HOW WE LIVED

By Peter Farrar

The Korean people and their country on the eve of war

In 1950, the Koreans were a poor but proud people. They had their own language, a unique phonetic alphabet of 28 simple characters and a tradition of civilized culture going back for over a thousand years. Unfortunately, the kingdom of Korea failed to modernise quickly in the late nineteenth century and was seized by Japan, which ruled the country until the defeat of 1945. Then came a second misfortune, the temporary division of the country into two zones as the result of a tacit compromise by the United States and Russia, both fearing each other's political and military influence over the whole country.

The division greatly hindered the economic development of the country, since most of the manufacturing industry, mines and power generation was in the north, while the south had big agricultural resources, especially rice. But everywhere the heart of the people was in the countryside of small villages, cottages made of wood and mud and thatched with straw. Oxen pulled ploughs in the paddy fields, often smelly from the use of night soil as a fertilizer. Men and women dressed mainly in white clothes, kept amazingly white by the women who beat them with wood at the river's edge. Men carried loads on A-shaped frames; women carried loads on their heads and babies on their backs. Roads were rough dirt tracks. In the south, a railway went from Pusan to Seoul. It became familiar to British troops in the war, who from mid 1951 used the terminus at Tokchon, north of Seoul.

The war came as a cruel blow to the Korean people who had not much wealth but their lives to lose and separation from their families, sometimes for ever. British soldiers and sailors first saw the Korean people in their misery. Thirty years later, some were able to return and found a country transformed. It was a splendid opportunity to meet the people on equal terms and learn about their achievements and modern way of life.

Why the United Nations took action

When the North Korean army, with Russian built tanks and weapons, swept over the 38th parallel into South Korea on 27th June 1950, it was judged by the United States, Britain and other powers, and, not least, by the Secretary-General of the U.N. as a direct challenge to the authority of the U.N. and also as a test by the Soviet Russia of the Western will to resist. It was in that spirit that Britain immediately placed her Far Eastern fleet under U.S. Naval Command and later sent troops.

The Korean War came when the international outlook was already grim. The Cold War was at its height. Eastern Europe was under firm Russian control. West Berlin had very narrowly escaped this fate during the Russian blockade of 1948-49. In 1949, the Chinese Communists triumphed in China, and it seemed that Russia had got a potentially powerful ally. The North Atlantic Alliance was formed under American leadership. The U.N. was only five years old and although disagreements between the West and the Eastern bloc hindered the proper working of the U.N., there was still much confidence that it could be a more effective organisation than its predecessor, the League of Nations.

In 1947 the intractable problem of how to unite Korea was placed in the hands of the U.N. by the United States. A U.N. Temporary Commission on Korea was established which tried to supervise elections in 1948 in North and South Korea, prior to the formation of a united government. But the Commission members were not allowed into North Korea. After elections in South Korea, observed by the Commission, the great majority of U.N. member states voted to recognise the sole legality of the South Korean government in the peninsula. The South Korean government, under President Syngman Rhee, was thus a ward of the U.N.

In June 1950, the Republic had a small army but without tanks and heavy artillery. By contrast, the North Korean army had Russian T34 tanks, heavy artillery and a small airforce. It would have conquered South Korea were it not for the fact that the United States had occupation forces (although very under-strength and under equipped) in Japan which were mobilised to assist South Korea. Very quickly, the Security Council of the U.N. authorised military assistance to South Korea. It was fortunate that Russia, which could have vetoed the Resolutions, was then boycotting the Security Council because the Nationalist Chinese delegate had not been replaced by one from Communist China. Within a few weeks, fifteen countries had promised forces to fight in Korea alongside the Americans and South Koreans, and five others promised medical units. It was a unique operation of the U.N., unlikely ever to be repeated.

Soon after General MacArthur's landings at Inchon on 15th September 1950, the battered remnants of the North Korean army fled north of the 38th parallel, ignoring a call for surrender. On 7th October 1950, the U.N. General Assembly passed a Resolution declaring that Korea should be united under U.N. auspices. Unfortunately, Communist China decided to intervene in order to save the North Korean army from complete destruction and also perhaps to drive out U.N. forces from Korea. In November 1950, Britain tried to get a pause in the fighting to allow time for talks with the Chinese aimed at a peaceful achievement of Korean unity. A secret plan for a buffer zone between the Yalu river and the U.N. forces was put to the United States but it was rejected. The subsequent fighting turned the war into a long indecisive struggle. The armistice of 27th July 1953 left Korea divided at roughly the 38th Parallel where it had begun. Nevertheless, the prosperous and fast developing modern state in the south, the Republic of Korea, exists as a result of the U.N. effort in 1950-53.

The war made only a small impact on the British public partly because the total size of British forces involved at any one time was small - not more than 15,000 soldiers and 7,000 sailors - and partly because reporting was confined to brief coverage in the cinema newsreels and newspapers. There was nothing like the impact of T.V. reportage of the Vietnam War fifteen years later. But the political and military lessons of the first "limited war" of this century continue to be important and ought to be more widely studied than they have been.

Those who served

When the war began, Britain had troops widely dispersed in Europe, the Middle East and Far East (Malaya and Hong Kong). There were no reserves for dispatch to

Korea. The army needed National Servicemen to maintain its strength. In June 1950, the period of service was eighteen months from the age of eighteen. The war obliged the Attlee government to raise it to two years in order to meet the army's needs. A longer period was also required by the fact that soldiers had to be aged at least nineteen for service in the Korean War. This measure would take many months before it made a real difference. But the Navy was almost totally manned by Regulars. With 22 ships in the Far East in June, 1950, and several in Japanese waters, it was able to give immediate help.

Britain initially promised an independent brigade for Korea but it had to be reinforced, equipped and trained. In the meantime, so desperate was the situation in Korea - by mid-July 1950 U.N. and South Korean forces were confined to the Pusan perimeter - that two infantry battalions were sent from the Hong Kong garrison at the end of August. Eventually, 29 Independent Brigade with tanks and artillery sailed from Britain at the beginning of October 1950. It was composed of Regulars, Reservists (men recalled from civilian life) and National Servicemen.

A total of fifteen infantry battalions, four tank regiments, four artillery regiments and many other supporting units, served in the Korean War (see Appendix No. 1). The average tour of duty of an infantry battalion was one year. But there was a continuous flow of National Service drafts to and from units. To keep these going, several troopships sailed back and forth between Britain and Pusan. H.M.T. *Empire Halladale, Empire Fowey, Empire Orwell, Empire Pride, Empire Windrush, Dilwara, Asturias* and others became familiar names to the troops. The voyage averaged five or six weeks with brief shore leave at Aden, Colombo, Singapore and Hong Kong. Sometimes drafts went to the Battle Training School at Haramura, near Kure, Japan. Occasionally, reinforcements were flown from Britain. Early in September 1950, 200 men of 41 Independent Commando, Royal Marines, were flown to Japan for training prior to active operations.

By 1952, two-thirds at least of battalions were composed of National Servicemen. They fought remarkably well and grumbled no more than Regular soldiers normally do. There were many reasons for this. The World War had ended recently enough for all men to be used to fathers or brothers serving in the forces and indeed conscription had continued without a break since 1945. The British people were also thoroughly used to having their troops in trouble-spots all over the world. The National Serviceman expected to be sent anywhere and knew that duty had to be done. He was also, as a child of the World War and post-war austerity years, accustomed to food and sweets rationing and luxury goods being scarce and expensive. The gap between life on active service and civilian life was not so great as it would be today. And, of course, the vast majority of National Servicemen were unmarried, and so there was very little disruption of family life.

What soldiers thought about the war politically is difficult to assess accurately. The War Office produced a little booklet *Notes on Korea* in August 1950 (reprinted as *Korea* in 1952) which gave basic facts about U.N. participation in the war and about the country. Some units received it and some did not. In any case, it is unlikely that the average soldier read much of it. There was probably a general and vague feeling that the war had been caused by Communist trouble-makers and that Britain had (as usual) volunteered to do something about it. In the front-line there was little discussion of politics. Physical toil was too wearing and mental activity was reserved for thoughts of food, beer, sleep, home and girlfriends. During the static war from November 1951, the enemy left leaflets on front-line wire urging soldiers to surrender or demand peace. They had no effect but were often kept as souvenirs.

Korea - illustrating British operations

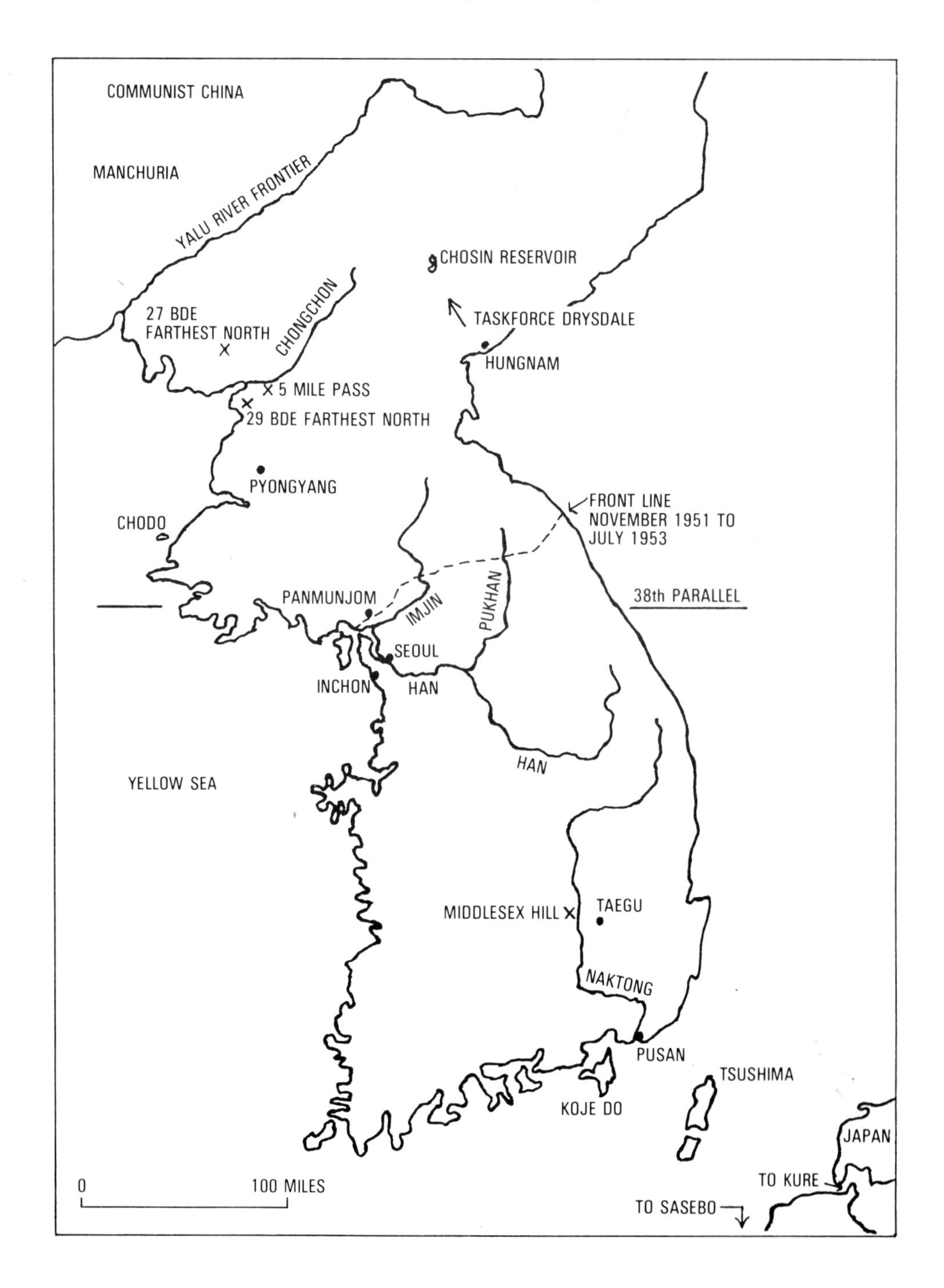

What the army and Royal Marines achieved, 1950-51

Until the formation of the Commonwealth Division in July 1951, British army units were grouped in two brigades which fought separately under higher American command. On 29th August 1950, 27 Brigade - an emergency and under-strength brigade composed of the 1 Bn. Middlesex Regiment and the 1 Bn. Argyll and Sutherland Highlanders - arrived from Hong Kong. Soon it was joined by 3 Bn. Royal Australian Regiment and in February 1951 by 1 Bn. Princess Patricia's Canadian Light Infantry. It was commanded by Brigadier B. A. Coad D.S.O. & Bar. Until 16 Field Regiment Royal New Zealand Artillery joined in December 1950, it relied on American artillery support and on American tank support all the time.

In early November 1950, 29 Independent Brigade Group, commanded by Brigadier T. Brodie D.S.O., arrived from Britain. It consisted of 1 Bn. Gloucestershire Regiment, 1 Bn. Royal Northumberland Fusiliers, 1 Bn. Royal Ulster Rifles, 45 Field Regiment Royal Artillery, 170 Independent Mortar Battery R.A. (with 4.2 inch mortars), 11 (Sphinx) Light Anti-Aircraft Battery (with Bofors guns), 8 King's Royal Irish Hussars (with the magnificent new Centurion tanks), C Squadron 7 Royal Tank Regiment (with Churchill flame throwing tanks known as Crocodiles), and 55 Field Squadron Royal Engineers.

The two brigades did not total more than 15,000 men, compared with the American army of 120,000 men in November 1950. But their quality gave them an importance out of all proportion to their numbers. They had a large proportion of officers and men who had experience of war in 1939-45. They had a good traditional training in which marching and digging as well as shooting played a big part. 27 Brigade came from the hills of the New Territory of Hong Kong, a good preparation for Korea. British soldiers were used to strict discipline and imbued with regimental pride that was proof against any adversity. The small size and esprit de corps of the two brigades made them very useful for independent roles.

The Argylls and Middlesex helped to defend the Pusan perimeter and attacked across the Naktong river in September 1950, for which it was awarded the Presidential Unit Citation of the Republic of Korea. Major K. Muir (Argylls) was postumously awarded the Victoria Cross. In October, 27 Brigade was given the task of leading the advance of U.N. forces into N. Korea. It was relieved by an American unit on 30th October 1950 at Chongju, forty miles from the Yalu. It was not given an offensive role in MacArthur's drive to the Yalu from 24th November because Britain had been assured by the U.S. Joint Chiefs of Staff that its troops would not, for political reasons, be deployed nearer than thirty miles to the Yalu.

But when the hugh Chinese army (much larger than MacArthur thought) launched its counter - offensive, forcing U.N. forces to retreat, 27 Brigade became a rearguard unit. On 29th and 30th November 1950, the Middlesex, with five American tanks and a battery of 105mm. guns, held the southern end of a five mile pass through the mountains south of Kunu-ri. They were able to help large numbers of wounded men of the badly mauled U.S. 2 Division coming out of the pass. 29 Brigade, which arrived in Korea in early November, was rushed to the north of Pyongyang but was soon ordered south again in the wake of the general retreat.

Away to the east, 41 Independent Commando Royal Marines played a valiant part in the fighting retreat of the U.S. 1 Marine Division from the Chosin Reservoir to Hungnam on the coast and evacuation. The U.S. Marines were awarded the Presidential Unit Citation in 1953 but 41 Commando had to wait until 1957 because until then regulations excluded foreign units from receiving the U.S. Navy award.

This was not the case with the Army award, the Distinguished Unit Citation, often called inaccurately the P.U.C. The fact that 41 Commando was disbanded in 1952 had no bearing on the matter, although its reformation in 1960 did permit the presentation of the Battle Streamer in 1961.

In January 1951, the Chinese launched another great offensive which carried them sixty miles south of the 38th parallel. 27 and 29 Brigades made a fighting retreat. Ten miles north-west of Seoul, 29 Brigade was nearly cut off by the clever outflanking attacks of the Chinese. The Royal Ulster Rifles were the hardest hit in a narrow valley, from which they escaped with much loss.

In February and March 1951, U.N. forces pushed the enemy back over the 38th Parallel, but in April the Chinese and North Koreans made yet another powerful offensive to regain what they had recently lost. 29 Brigade resistance in the Battle of the Imjin of 22-25 April seriously delayed the enemy advance and saved Seoul from a third capture. 29 Brigade held a sector of great strategic importance along the southern bank of the Imjin, for behind it lay one of the main routes to Seoul. It was doubly important because the line curved northwards on the Brigade's right flank. If the Brigade front collapsed, the American units to the north-east could be cut off.

29 Brigade had been reinforced by the Belgian volunteer battalion, but even so, it was obliged to hold key hill positions rather than a continuously defended line. The strategy of 1 Corps was to "roll with the punch" but it meant that 29 Brigade in the western sector had to conduct the slowest fighting retreat, allowing quicker withdrawals by the troops to the east. The Gloucesters on the left of the Brigade were the pivot of a retreating line of troops. They had to stay put in an isolated group of hills. Only within this strategic context does the four day stand and inevitable surrender of the Gloucesters have its full meaning and justification. But equally important was the slow fighting retreat of the Royal Northumberland Fusiliers, the Royal Ulster and the Belgians.If they had not done this successfully, the sacrifice of the Gloucesters would have been pointless, as the Chinese would have poured through any gap opened up.

Colonel J. P. Carne D.S.O., the commanding officer of the Gloucesters, and Lieutenant P.K.E. Curtis, Duke of Cornwall's Light Infantry attached to the Gloucesters, were awarded the Victoria Cross, Curtis posthumously. The 1 Bn. Gloucestershire Regiment and C Troop 170 Mortar Battery R.A., and the Belgian battalion, were awarded Distinguished Unit Citations by President Truman. The R. Northumberland Fusiliers and the R. Ulster Rifles, who suffered heavy casualties, deserved to be included. Colonel K.O.N. Foster of R.N.F. was killed.

To the east of Seoul, 27 Brigade fought another blocking battle at Kapyong. The Australian and Canadian battalions had the main part, the Middlesex in support.

The Commonwealth Division

The Commonwealth Division was not formed until July 1951 because there were not until then enough forces available. The arrival of two more Canadian battalions in May 1951 was a big help. The Division was now made up of 25 Canadian Brigade with its own Sherman tanks and field artillery, 29 British Brigade and 28 Commonwealth Brigade. The latter replaced 27 Brigade but inherited the New Zealand field artillery and 60 Indian Field Ambulance. The Divisional Commanders were all British - Maj. Gen. A. J. H. Cassels D.S.O. (1951-52), Maj. Gen. M. M. A. R. West D.S.O. (1951-53) and (after the armistice) Maj. Gen. H. Murray D.S.O. (1953-54). Three Australians held the administrative Command of British Commonwealth Forces Korea: Lt. Gen. Sir H. Robertson D.S.O. (1950-51),

Lt. Gen. W. Bridgeford M.C. (1951-53) and Lt. Gen. H. Wells D.S.O. (1953-54). Three weeks before the division was formed, cease-fire talks began at Kaesong on 10th July 1951 (later transferred to Panmunjom) but it took two years of wrangling and much more fighting before it was achieved. Not until the end of October 1951, did the enemy, who argued for a restoration of the 38th parallel, accept that the battle line should be the demarcation line after the cease-fire. In the meantime, the Commonwealth Division made its first and only divisional scale offensive as part of Operation Commando. It achieved the objective of pushing the line north of the Imjin and capturing the massive Kowang San hill feature known to the army as 355 (height in metres) or Little Gibraltar, and also Maryang San (Point 317). But during November 1951 the Chinese repeatedly fought to regain Maryang San from the Royal Northumberland Fusiliers, Leicesters, King's Own Scottish Borderers and King's Shropshire Light Infantry. During this fighting, Private W. Speakman, Black Watch attached to K.O.S.B., won the Victoria Cross. The Chinese finally succeeded but 355 was held.

From now onwards the Commonwealth Division held a line stretching eight miles from 355 to just west of the Samichon river. In October 1952, this left flank was extended a little to include the Hook feature, a complex juncture of ridges. Until the cease-fire of July 1953, the Division repulsed all attacks on these two vitally important features guarding the best routes to Seoul. The Chinese attacks on the Hook in November 1952 and May 1953, when it was held by the Black Watch and Duke of Wellington's Regiment respectively, were the most notable against British troops.

The war between November 1951 and July 1953 has been called "the static war". It may have been so geographically, but not for the soldiers manning the line of fortified hills and ridges. The work of patrolling, raiding, digging, wiring, laying mines never ceased. The Chinese were clever soldiers and had good intelligence of Commonwealth units, sometimes welcomed by name by loudspeakers at points where the lines were close. Their evident foreknowledge of a raid by two platoons of the Royal Fusiliers (City of London Regt.) in November 1952 led to a costly ambush.

Fortunately, the enemy did not attempt to dispute U.N. air control of the battle line, but they used mortars and artillery to good effect. It was presumably the increasing volume of shells and mortar bombs which prompted the Divisional order in September 1952 for steel helmets to be worn forward of battalion H.Q. Hitherto, jungle hats in summer and assorted soft headgear in winter had been the norm. Another effort to keep casualties to the minimum was the introduction for patrol use of nylon armoured vests (waistcoats). They weighed 8lbs. and could stop "burp" sub-machine gun bullets except at close range. The Division received 860 vests between August and November 1952. Swift evacuation of wounded by helicopter also did much to reduce deaths. The number of men killed in action in the first five battalions during the war of movement averaged seventy each; it was forty for each of the ten battalions which came after.

Infantry weapons were those of the Second World War - the 303 Rifle No. 4, the Bren LMG, the Vickers Machine-Gun, the Sten and the 3 inch mortar. Until February 1953, the Divisional artillery was limited to 25 pounder guns. But then the British 74 Medium Battery (guns with a much longer range) arrived and initially supported the Americans while the Division was out of the line for two months. As part of the U.S. I Corps, the Division had the support of the American heavy artillery, including the 8 inch "Persuaders". A Royal Artillery weapon which really came into its own in Korea was the mobile 4.2 inch mortar. This had the capacity to lob bombs over high hills.

The Commonwealth Division area, 1951-53

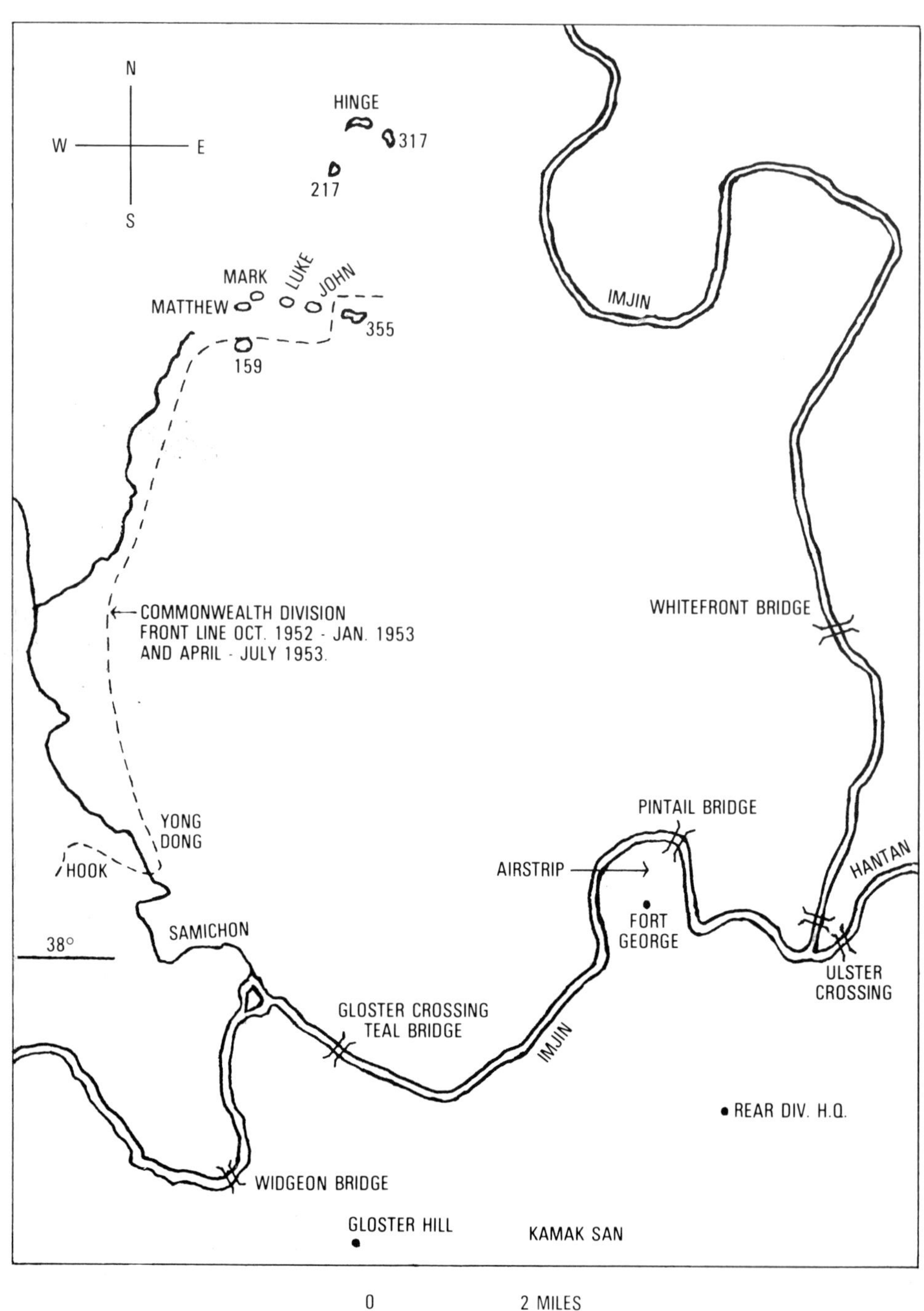

Tanks became artillery in the static war. They were entrenched hull down (to protect vulnerable tracks) on the tops of hills. The Centurion was very suited to hill climbing and strongly armoured. It fired a 20 pound shell.

The country occupied by the Commonwealth Division was a desolate wilderness of hills divided by the Imjin river over which American engineers constructed several high-level bridges of different kinds e.g. Teal and Whitefront (wooden trestle) and Parker Memorial (steel uprights). British troops persisted in calling the latter Pintail, the name of the floating bridge it replaced. In January 1953, a new low level Teal bridge on steel piles was opened to replace the trestle bridge destroyed by the monsoon river floods of 1952.

Civilians had been evacuated from the Divisional area. There were abandoned paddy fields and ruined villages of thatched mud built cottages. The soldiers' contacts with Koreans were confined almost entirely to three groups: (1) the hundred or so Korean Service Corps porters attached to each battalion, who dug trenches and bunkers and carried food and ammunition; (2) the Korean boys who did washing and other chores for officers and senior N.C.O.s in exchange for food, clothing and shelter; (3) the hundred KATCOM (Korean Augmentation Troops Commonwealth Division) soldiers who were fully integrated with each battalion in March 1953. They wore British uniform and ate ordinary British rations, but were paid by the R.O.K. Army.

The Royal Navy

Throughout the war, the Royal Navy had an important responsibility as part of the west coast blockade force, made up of Commonwealth ships. The east coast was blockaded by the U.S. Navy. There was a periodical exchange of ships by the two forces. The three successive west coast commanders were all Royal Navy officers: Rear Admirals W.G. Andrewes K.B.E., C.B., C.B.E., D.S.O., A.K. Scott-Moncrieff K.C.B., C.B., C.B.E., D.S.O. and E.G.A. Clifford K.C.B, O.B.E. The navy had six main tasks : to prevent the enemy using his ports, at least by big ships; to keep the many islands off the west coast in U.N. hands; to bombard railways, roads, bridges and other installations; to land raiding parties; to attack similar targets by the Fleet Air Arm of the light carrier; to pick up ditched pilots at sea and sometimes by helicopter on land.

The role of the navy could not be spectacular because it had neither an enemy fleet nor airforce to contend with. The North Koreans had a small airforce which was soon destroyed but not before H.M.S. *Comus,* a destroyer, was badly holed on 23 August 1950 by a near miss bomb from a Russian built Ilyushin 10 bomber. Later, Chinese aircraft based in Manchuria did not attack warships but sometimes attacked aircraft from the carriers. The main enemy hazards were mines laid by fishing boats and shore batteries. Luckily, the mines were out of date Russian make and fairly easy to sweep. In winter, the Yellow Sea was subjected to ice floes and freezing inshore. Working conditions on ships were often dangerous and exhausting.

Four British light carriers, *Triumph, Theseus, Glory* and *Ocean* served in turn off the west coast. The Australian light carrier H.M.A.S. *Sydney* also did a stint. There was usually an American light carrier as well, making up a normal force of two carriers in the Yellow Sea. One squadron of Seafires, five of Sea Furies and five of Fireflies flew from the four British carriers during the war. The Royal Navy lost about 45 officers and ratings, mostly Fleet Air Arm.

The Royal Air Force

Two R.A.F. squadrons of Sunderland flying boats were stationed at Iwakuni, Japan. They did much transport work. The Commonwealth Division had the assistance of two R.A.F. Flights of Austers (light observation aircraft) - 1903 Independent Air Observation Post Flight and 1913 Light Liaison Flight. The former had the task of spotting for the artillery; the latter had tasks including general reconnaissance of the enemy lines. Besides Austers, it had one Cessna L-19 for use by the Divisional Commander. The pilots of both Flights were Army and the ground staff were Army and R.A.F.

A number of R.A.F. pilots flew fighter planes through attachment to the Australian 77 Fighter Squadron and the American 16 Fighter Interception Squadron of 51 Fighter Interception Wing. The Australian squadron was supplied with the British Meteor jet fighter. Five British pilots were killed in action in 1952-53. The British pilots with the American squadron flew F86 Sabre jets.

Peacekeeping Forces

The cease-fire of July 1953 has never been followed by a peace treaty and the U.N. Command still exists. In 1953-54, there was a danger of a recurrence of fighting. Until October 1954, the Commonwealth Division manned the fortified line behind the four kilometre wide demilitarised zone separating the opposed armies. Then a reduction of forces began until only a Commonwealth Contingent remained in 1956-57. The 1 Bn. Royal Sussex Regiment, the last British battalion in Korea, left Inchon on H.M.T. *Asturias* on 27 July 1957, bringing to an end the seven year period during which the British army had been present.

Food and health in the army

Rations in the front line usually consisted of American C7 packs with tea and bread from Field Bakeries. The C7 was a cardboard box containing canned rations for one man for 24 hours. There were several varieties of "main course", for example, ham and lima beans, pork and beans, frankfurter chunks and beans, meatballs and corned beef hash - the last being the least popular. There were also tins of fruit, salted crackers, biscuits, chocolate, chewing gum, cigarettes, coffee and dried milk sachets, toilet paper and a tiny tin opener. Solid fuel tablets were placed on a little frame in order to heat the tins. Issued separately, from 1952, there were American self-heating tins of soup, a boon on some patrols and at other times.

When units were in reserve areas, there was a chance for the cooks to set up their kitchens. Meals were then usually a combination of fresh rations and canned items from British ten-men Compo packs.

Health was generally good. The most dangerous disease was haemorrhagic fever, but fortunately its victims were few. In 1952, there were 94 cases in the Commonwealth forces, of whom three died. Malaria was the biggest potential danger, for there were abandoned paddy fields everywhere in the fighting areas, perfect breeding places for mosquitos. But, by a strange paradox, Paludrine tablets, in use since 1946, partly removed the problem from Korea to Britain. The second edition of the War Office booklet *Korea* (printed in May 1952) stated that, if taken daily, "the drug will prevent you from developing malaria". What was not generally known in the army was that the malaria parasite (Plasmodium Vivax in Korea) could enter into the liver or spleen and stay dormant until after the Paludrine course ended, normally towards the end of the voyage home. Some demobbed soldiers went down with malaria for the first time in Britain, and usually did not realise (as in the writer's case) what their illness was. In 1952 there were 195 cases of malaria in the Commonwealth forces in Korea.

Venereal disease was caught by a proportion of soldiers, usually on leave in Japan. But there is no readily available evidence as to what types of VD were most common. Treatment was prompt and men were not off duty.

There was severe cold in the winter. Troops in the first winter of 1950-51 were glad to get extra items of clothing and headgear from the Americans, but from the winter of 1951-52 special British winter clothing was issued. This consisted of a string vest, long johns, under-trousers, trousers, parka with a wired hood, and thick rubber-soled boots. Puttees were worn throughout the year. Sleeping bags were issued but were not used in the front-line because of the time needed to get out of them in an emergency.

The dug-outs of various kinds, known as "hoochies" or "bashas" were heated with "chuffers", ammunition boxes into which petrol dripped from a copper tube fed from a can fixed high on the outside. Chimneys were made from shell cases. Diesel oil was the official fuel but it flowed too sluggishly to be any good. The chuffers often caused fires, especially in tents. In camps with large tents, American space heaters burning diesel were used.

News, entertainment and leave in the army

Mail from home took seven to ten days by air. In November 1950, 29 Brigade produced the cyclostyled newsheet *Circle News,* named from the white circle flash. From 8 October 1951, this was replaced by the *Crown News* in an identical format but serving the whole Commonwealth Division. Another newsheet, the *Korean Base Gazette* was produced at Pusan. After the war, in 1954, the *Seoul City Spectator,* a more ambitious newsheet with photographs was printed in Seoul. Two newspapers not produced by British forces also circulated, the *Japan News* and the *Pacific Stars and Stripes*.

Depending on access to the signallers' wireless sets, a news bulletin from Britain could be heard at 2210 hours via Britcom Broadcasting Station at Kure in Japan. There was an Auxiliary Station at Iwakuni.

Regiments had canteens at 'A' Echelon about two miles behind the line. Japanese Asahi beer was standard. There were film shows in the open, even in the winter. The NAAFI/EFI toured with mobile vans and built "inns" on the main supply routes e.g. Newmarket Roadhouse, Ship Inn. Periodically, well-known entertainers came with a small group from Britain e.g. Brian Reece in 1951, Ted Ray and Frankie Howerd in 1952. The female singers e.g. Helen Ward, Eve Boswell, Carole Carr were warmly appreciated by us in the sternly masculine front line.

Every soldier was entitled to three days Rest and Recuperation leave at a tented camp near Inchon and five days at Ebisu hotel in Tokyo.

War cemeteries and memorials

The majority of British dead were buried in the U.N. Memorial Cemetery outside

Pusan. It was established by the U.N. Command on 18 January, 1951, when burials began and some remains transferred from earlier, temporary cemeteries. It is now administered by a special U.N. Commission. In 1965, a memorial was built within the cemetery commemorating those with no known graves. A number of men were buried in the British Cemetery, Yokahama, Japan.

In July 1951, the R. Ulster Rifles built a stone memorial near the valley north-west of Seoul where so many men had been killed in January 1951. After the war it was taken to Ballymena, Northern Ireland, and re-erected. In 1957, the R. Sussex Regt. and the Royal Engineers built a memorial to the Gloucesters and C Troop, 170 Mortar Battery, R.A. on the hillside of Solma-ri - Hill 235 - south of the Imjin river. It was unveiled by the R. Sussex commanding officer and the British ambassador on 19 June 1957.

In 1961, a window depicting Saint George and the Dragon - representing the Commonwealth forces - was placed in the Anglican Cathedral in Seoul. It was made by Harry Stammers. The Cathedral built in the 1920's luckily escaped destruction in the Korean War. In 1967, the South Koreans built a monument at Kapyong to commemorate the Battle of Kapyong in April 1951.

Gloucester Cathedral displays the little stone cross carved by Colonel Carne V.C., D.S.O. of the Gloucestershire Regiment during his captivity in North Korea. The style is that of the ancient Celtic cross to be seen in Cornwall, his native county.

A memorial dedicated to all British servicemen who died in the war was erected in the crypt of St. Paul's Cathedral in 1987. The Book of Remembrance, when completed, will contain the names of over one thousand men who died while serving in British forces.

Chapter 2

THE NAKTONG RIVER AND "MIDDLESEX HILL", SEPTEMBER, 1950.

By Colonel Andrew M. Man, DSO, OBE.

When General Walker, the United Nations Commander, started his counter-offensive in Korea from the Taegu/Pusan bridgehead on September 16th 1950, the 27th British Infantry Brigade consisting of Brigade Headquarters and two Battalions only, the 1st Middlesex Regiment and the 1st Argyll and Sutherland Highlanders, both from Hong Kong, supported by United States tanks and artillery, and assisted by South Korean Police levies, were holding some ten thousand yards of front along the River Naktong to the south west of Taegu. They had no part of play in the initial breakout, but were later instructed to make plans for an assault crossing of the River Naktong to the south of Waegwan, with a view to outflanking any enemy holding up the main advance through that town.

Later, this order was cancelled, and fresh instructions were issued for the immediate release of the Brigade in the River Naktong position by a tired United States Battalion, and for the Brigade's concentration east of the Naktong some eight miles south of Waegwan, as reserve to the 24th United States Infantry Division. This division had just returned to the line after its rearguard action against the advancing North Koreans almost unaided from Pyongyang to Taegu.

By early morning of the 21st September this relief was complete, and by 11.00 hours the 1st Middlesex, the leading unit, was arriving at its concentration area, a mile to the east of the river in a wide valley overlooked by the hills on the west of the river; an unfortunate circumstance, this overlooking, as events were later to prove.

Before proceeding further, it would not be a bad idea to take a look at this Middlesex Battalion, whose first action in Korea is about to be described. They had left Hong Kong for Pusan in Korea at five days notice only; arriving in H.M.S. *Unicorn* on 29th August. Although it had been categorically stated that no troops would be taken from Hong Kong for service in Korea, there were few soldiers who did not have a feeling that they would be called upon to serve in that country. But even if it had been necessary to prepare in advance for such an eventuality, there would have been no cause for any change in current thought or training, in view of the similarity of the Hong Kong and Korean terrain. Before leaving, it had been necessary to accept some hundred and fifty Other Ranks from other Battalions in Hong Kong, to bring the Battalion up to strength of three rifle companies, each of 120 Other Ranks, and a Headquarter Company, which included a 3 inch Mortar and a Medium Machine-Gun Platoon. In Officers, the Battalion was complete without any outside assistance. Some 55% of all Other Ranks were National Service soldiers all of them over nineteen years of age, but very few with more than six months service with the Battalion.

Training in Hong Kong had been hard and continuous among hills and paddy fields under difficult climatic conditions, so that a high standard of man-management, in particular, had been reached. Morale was very high. On arrival in Korea, the Middlesex Regiment spent some five days shaking-down and receiving vehicles, followed by some two weeks in a quiet corner of the line, patrolling and practicing digging-in and other aspects of defensive warfare training.

Very soon after his arrival ahead of the Battalion, the Commanding Officer met the Brigade Commander, who told him that so far from being somewhere in the rear, the Brigade was likely to be shelled at any time by North Korean artillery west of the river. The sound of shellfire certainly seemed very close, and there was a noticeable quickening of effort on the part of all who had so far arrived to dig themselves in. The Commanding Officer was ordered to go at once to a United States Battalion Headquarters some thousand yards off and just short of the river, to learn the plight of the 24th United States Division Reconnaissance Company who, with tanks, were in trouble some three miles to the west of the river, and who would probably have to be assisted by him and his Battalion that day, in accordance with instructions to be given later.

The Commanding Officer set off in his jeep for the small knoll on which the United States Battalion Headquarters were located, where he learned that a United States Reconnaissance Company had crossed the river by ferry the previous day with some tanks, in order to cover the left flank of the main advance east of the river. They were now held up in a small hamlet by mortar and S.P. fire. The hills, dominating further movement, were reported to be held by enemy infantry, and the road on the west of the river, by which they had come, was likely to be cut at any time. No other friendly troops were, as yet, over the river, with the exception of a small detachment who were too far away and near the river to be of any assistance. It appeared, also, that the ferry was no longer functioning, owing to accurate shellfire, and that an extremely rickety footbridge was being shelled at frequent intervals by artillery so far unlocated. The Commanding Officer spoke by wireless to the Reconnaissance Company Commander, arranging for tanks to meet him and his Recce party at 16.15 hours at the west end of this rickety bridge, subject to confirmation later, and warned the Company Commander that, in the event of these orders being confirmed, his Reconnaissance Company would come under the orders of the Commanding Officer of the Middlesex Regiment, that is, himself.

After looking at the bridge, the Commanding Officer returned to his Battalion and put his Company Commanders in the picture. At about 14.00 hours, the Brigade Commander ordered the Middlesex to go to the assistance of this Reconnaissance Company, crossing the river at 17.00 hours that day or, if possible, earlier, and to make good the two hills which dominated the advance of the Company, to be known later as "Middlesex Hill", on the right, and Point 282 on the left. He confirmed that the United States Reconnaissance Company would come under his command, and told him that a Company of the 1st Argyll and Sutherland Highlanders would, that night, secure a hill feature to the west of the bridge.

The Middlesex were to be supported by a battery of 105 MM guns, from whom a Forward Observation officer was being despatched with instructions to report to the Commanding Officer west of the bridge. This officer, however, never appeared; probably due to an order, then in force in the United States Army, forbidding Artillery Observation parties to move by night.

By 16.00 hours all orders had been issued for the movement of the Battalion on foot over the river; to be followed as and when practicable by vehicles, mortars and other essential but non-portable equipment, under the orders of the Battalion Second-in-Command, Major R. A. Gwyn. At that time, the Commanding Officer and his Company Commanders, with a Platoon of 'A' Company, crossed the bridge - a most unsafe operation - though not because of the enemy who, strangely enough were, at that moment, inactive. The waiting tanks were boarded and the party moved off the road. At first, on either side, there was evidence of fighting - bodies and burnt-out houses - and throughout the short journey, one felt exposed and unprotected; a feeling which solitary, United States tanks, stationed infrequently in the valley, along the road, with crews looking anything by happy, did little to dispel.

The United States Reconnaissance Company Commander was met at the hamlet, which he had closely surrounded with his armoured personnel carriers and his tanks, his Infantry - some twenty or thirty strong - being entrenched on the small hill overlooking the hamlet, some hundred yards from it. He pointed out Point 282 and "Middlesex Hill", which appeared to look right down and into his position, and from which the accurate mortaring of his Company was being directed. The Middlesex Officers were struck by the very concentrated dispositions of this Company in the hamlet. They could hardly have been sited more closely together, or have presented a more worthwhile mortar target. On enquiry, they were told that only in this way could the maximum protection be provided for the crews, who expected to be attacked by creeping enemy patrols with hand-grenades. The Reconnaisance Company Commander himself, and his Headquarters, were with their jeeps on the road in the centre of the hamlet. After a quick recce of the hamlet and around the foothills, five hundred yards to the front, in an atmosphere of expectancy and almost of eeriness; while sporadic mortaring was occuring forward of the hamlet, in the paddy fields; the Commanding Officer decided that 'A' Company - Major D. B. Rendell, M.B.E., M.C. - who were leading, should move at once to Ridge X and make their way forward to occupy Ridge Y for the night, if it were free of the enemy. (See sketch map on page 18).

'D' Company, Major J. E. F. Willoughby commanding, were to take over Ridge X behind them, while 'B' Company, Major W. P. M. Allen, MC, commanding, with the United States Reconnaisance Company under command, for local defence, would that night be responsible for the protection of the hamlet area, and of the Battalion Tactical Headquarters to be located therein. The tanks, passed on the road and, further back, the Company of the Argyll and Sutherland Highlanders would, it was hoped, make it difficult for the road to be cut. Any change in the disposition of these tanks, at that late hour, would have been unwise.

Next morning, 'B' Company with 3 tanks was to capture "Plum Pudding Hill",a round feature as this name implies, some 300 feet high, starting at 07.00 hours. 'D' Company, supported by all the tanks in the hamlet, passing through 'A' Company on Ridge Y, was to assault and capture "Middlesex Hill" in accordance with orders to be issued later; any available artillery supporting this action.

It had now become clearly impracticable to do anything about Point 282 until "Plum Pudding Hill", and "Middlesex Hill", which immediately dominated the road and hamlet, were in our hands. By this time, about 18.00 hours, the marching Companies were arriving to the accompaniment of mortar fire, which was near enough to be uncomfortable, although no casualties were fortunately incurred.

It was a fine sight to see the way the men moved forward on either side of the road, apparently oblivious to the mortaring, particularly as it was the first time they - mostly National Servicemen - had come under shellfire. One Company Commander was heard to tell his men to lie down quietly at the side of the road and not to think it necessary to show their mettle by standing up, which would be foolish. That such an instruction was necessary was a tribute to the bearing of all, particularly in view of the obvious eagerness of the United States Reconnaissance

The Naktong River and Middlesex Hill

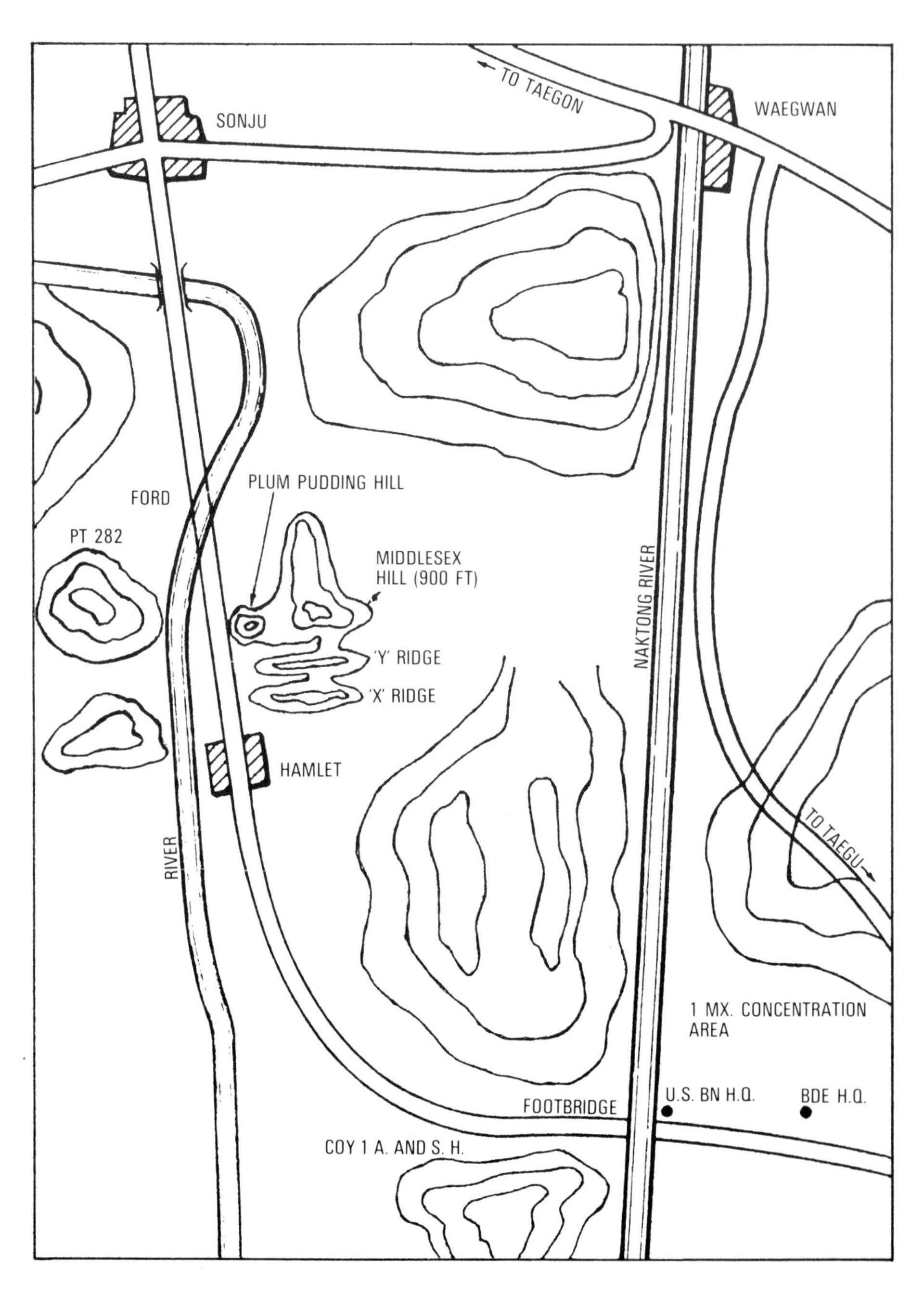

NOT TO SCALE

Company's soldiers around them to get to ground. These young, National Service soldiers were showing their mettle to good effect in this, their first experience of enemy fire.

Everything went according to plan: 'A' Company on Ridge Y, 'D' Company on Ridge X and 'A' Company with the United States Reconnaissance Company suitably disposed about the hamlet, all just before darkness fell. To the surprise of all, the night was uneventful, though bitterly cold, and the absence of non-portable stores meant that breakfast could not be much of a meal; in fact many went without. Before dawn, the Machine-Gun Platoon, Lieutenant G.G. Norton, arrived. They were destined to be of great value in the coming encounter.

Sharp at 07.00 hours the next morning, the leading Platoon of 'B' Company set off up the road to capture "Plum Pudding Hill". This they accomplished in fine fashion by the skilful use of ground, and a spirited bayonet charge, under the leadership of their Platoon Commander, Second Lieutenant Christopher Lawrence, who later was awarded the Military Cross. The tanks of the United States Reconnaissance Company did not place much reliance on the successful outcome of this action, and so steadfastly refused to advance further than some three hundred yards from the hamlet, whence they gave useful, though limited, covering fire. The capture of "Plum Pudding Hill" cost the North Koreans some twelve or more casualties, and brought about the abandonment, with their automatics, of a number of carefully sited machine-gun posts. Altogether, a most satisfactory start. The Platoon, unfortunately, lost three killed and three wounded.

Meanwhile, the Battalion Commander with one Officer had joined 'A' Company on Ridge Y with the Machine-Gun Platoon under 'A' Company command, whilst 'D' Company Commander was actively preparing for the assault of "Middlesex Hill," a ridge with very steep sides, some nine hundred feet high, from which a lot of small arms fire was coming. Incidentally, mortar fire was, by this time, landing frequently and accurately at the rear of Ridges X and Y and near the road, forward of the hamlet. One tank received a direct hit, and a number of Reconnaissance Company men became casualties. At about 09.30 hours, 'B' Company were ordered to consolidate "Plum Pudding Hill" and the adjacent ridge astride the road, and 'D' Company were instructed to put in their attack on "Middlesex Hill". 'A' Company, with the Machine-Gun Platoon, was to support this attack with the tanks in the hamlet area, whose fire was being co-ordinated by 'B' Company Commander, assisted by the Signals Officer, under the Battalion Commander's direction. In retrospect, a rather clumsy arrangement, though it worked rather well and made up, to a much greater extent than was expected, for the absence of artillery support, for which wireless messages to Brigade Headquarters, through main Battalion Headquarters, both still east of the river, were being constantly sent. Under cover of accurate, supporting fire from the tanks controlled in this way, the attack was launched along a saddle which, rising in a series of 'bumps', joined Ridge Y to "Middlesex Hill". When the leading Platoon of 'D' Company had made good the first of these 'bumps', some very accurate, medium shellfire fell on the crest of the objective, to the surprise of all.

'D' Company Commander, suspecting the Battalion Commander of arranging this without informing him, politely thanked him, and at the same time asked that it might by lifted to enable him to proceed. But nothing could be done, for no one knew whence it came - not even Brigade Headquarters, who were asked to do something about it, and quickly. Not long afterwards, however, 'B' Company Commander in the hamlet reported the arrival of a United States 155 mm Battery Observation party who, on climbing up to join the Battalion Commander on Ridge Y, in a somewhat heated state, denied allknowledge of the source of fire which was still coming down on the objective. These Artillery Officers, after considerable delay and much use of their wireless, discovered that a spotting plane was responsible for controlling the fire of another Battery of their Artillery Regiment upon this hill and, furthermore: "That so important a mission could, on no account, be stopped as a United States Reconnaissance Company was held up by enemy located thereon!" The Battalion Commander thereupon seized the microphone, identified himself, and explained with considerable restraint that the hill in question was, at that moment, being attacked by his soldiers who were assisting the Reconnaissance Company, now under his command and, added, that any further fire on this hill, unless with his permission, would directly effect the lives of British soldiers now held up in 'No-mans-land'. After a surprised and painful silence, a subdued 'Roger' was received, followed by a cessation of fire; whereupon 'D' Company continued the assault, supported as before with the tanks and Machine-Gun Platoon, whose shooting throughout was both accurate and effective.

The summit was reached after considerable physical effort in the hot sun, but without much interference from the enemy. Once reached, however, the leading Platoon Commander was killed and his men pinned to the ground by automatic fire from positions on the reverse slope, and on the backwards spur, whose existence hitherto was unknown. The despatch of the Artillery Observation party, who had at last managed to get their Batteries to take part in this operation, to join 'D' Company and one of the 'A' Company Platoons to take over that part of the objective, which was now in our hands, enabled the attack to continue with some really excellent shooting, a very short distance ahead of the forward troops from the 155 mm Battery.

By about 15.00 hours or, possibly, a little later, "Middlesex Hill" was in our hands, together with a number of Russian-pattern machine-guns, rifles, ammunition and rather more than a dozen enemy dead. While this action was in progress, both the attacking troops and 'B' Company on "Plum Pudding Hill" had seen large numbers of enemy 'making off' and discarding their uniforms. Upon these the guns were directed with good effect, so that enemy losses in killed and wounded must have been considerably greater than the actual number of bodies found would appear to show, particularly as the North Korean is always at pains to carry away with him, whenever possible, his dead and wounded. Our losses on "Middlesex Hill" were two killed and three wounded. Second Lieutenant G. A. White, the Platoon Commander who was killed, was awarded a postumous American Silver Star for his gallantry in this action.

That night, 'A' and 'B' Companies were entrenched on "Middlesex Hill", 'B' Company held "Plum Pudding Hill" astride the road, with Battalion Headquarters and the United States Reconnaissance Company acting as Battalion reserves in the hamlet area. That the enemy resented the loss of these positions, on which they had been well dug in, was proved by the artillery fire which he put down that night on the Middlesex positions, and by his mortaring of the area generally, which continued throughout the hours of daylight on both the first and second days of this operation. No doubt this fire was directed from Point 282, which was to be successfully attacked on the following day by the 1st Argyll and Sutherland Highlanders. This, it will be recalled, was the occasion when United States aircraft mistook them for enmy and attacked them with napalm bombs, causing a number of casualties.

The capture of their objective by the Middlesex now focused attention upon administration which, throughout the operation, had been a constant headache to the Battalion Second-in-Command on the east bank of the river. Enemy artillery had shown no signs of abating their offensive action in the bridge area. All attempts to repair the ferry enough to get vehicles across the river had, at first, been prevented, and had later been hindered as a result of his observation posts on the hill, and his guns, so carefully concealed, that no aircraft could find them. Brigade Headquarters had been forced to move back out of range and the Middlesex Rear Echelon was being considerably hampered in its efforts to get ammunition and food over the river to the forward Companies. In spite of this, the essential needs of the Battalion were got across and loaded onto the vehicles of the Reconnaissance Company for onward movement. Casualties were incurred in the bridge area by the Middlesex, including three men killed, and on all sides there was evidence of as high standard of devotion to duty as was to be found in the forward attacking Companies. As an example: Drummer G. Matthews of the Middlesex took over a raft with a defective motor, which he repaired, and with which he ferried over the river, in the face of considerable shellfire, all the mortar and other ammunition, which was immediately required forward. For this, he was later Mentioned-in-Despatches.

So occupied were the former elements of the Battalion, not only in attacking and then reorganising their position, but also in carrying water and food and other necessaries from the valley to the top of their hills, that it was some days before they realised that they could by no means claim a monopoly of enemy shellfire in the Battalion area as a whole.

Looking back on the operation, led by the Middlesex Battalion, it is possible to estimate the intention of the enemy who opposed them. Songju, a town some four miles further on than the hamlet, where the United States Reconnaissance Company had been held up, and to which the road through the hamlet led, was found to be the centre of a considerable gun area with large quantities of dumped ammunition. Its defence, therefore, was a matter of some importance to the enemy. To this end, the Point 282/"Middlesex Hill" line had to be held in some strength and, also, the approaches from Waegwan, as the Americans, later advancing from the town, discovered. The advancing United States Reconnaissance Company, therefore, had to be stopped. And, so for a time, it was. Further supplies for that Company, and reinforcements, must be hindered and harassed at the most suitable place, which was clearly the bridge area. Past experience had, however, led the North Koreans to believe that the Americans would be disinclined to leave the road. They were, therefore, content to sit passively on the hilltops once their positions had been dug, and even to leave the minimum troops thereon so that the maximum could sleep comfortably in the villages, on their own side of the position, until they were required to fight. Therein lay the seeds of their undoing, for there was evidence that the attacks on the Middlesex objectives had come as a surprise.

To the officers and men of the Middlesex Battalion, this action proved the value of the training they had undergone in Hong Kong, and gave conclusive evidence of the high morale under fire of the young, National Service soldier, of whom the Battalion was largely composed. It thus provided a splendid background for the future successes of the Battalion in Korea as part of the 27th British, later Commonwealth, Brigade. But it also had a wider significance than that: the watching Americans, for the first time, saw that enemy on hilltops could only be successfully removed by Infantry assaulting their positions. Aircraft, and guns and tanks located near roads, would always assist, but could never be substitutes for the foot soldier with his bayonet. When this lesson had been fully learned by them in Korea, the fortunes of the United Nations Forces improved considerably.

Chapter 3

THE 28TH BRITISH COMMONWEALTH BRIGADE IN THE BATTLE OF KOWANG SAN AND MARYANG SAN

By Brigadier G. Taylor, C.B.E., D.S.O., K.H.S.

Part 1 - Preliminary Plans

The Scene of War

Northward from the fast flowing Imjin River, which carves its way to the sea, through the lush greenery and the sultry blackness of craggy rocks and yellow sandstone hills, the country, till one meets the abrupt steepness of Kowang San, is with few exceptions a tangled area of low hillocks and ridges of little tactical significance. Where there is a sufficient depth of soil, these small features are covered with a semi-tropical growth, or with the foliage of dense clumps of pine and larch. During the summer this area had been dominated by the patrols of the British and Canadian Brigades, who had sallied out from their formidable and evergrowing defensive positions on the south bank of the Imjin River to harry and probe the enemy.

Towards the end of the rainy season in August, with the river falling rapidly, and in consequence no longer providing such a stout defensive barrier, it was decided to move the newly formed 1st Commonwealth Division over the river, and thereby straighten the 1st Corps line, much to the satisfaction of the 1st United States Cavalry Division on our right. The forward movement of the Division was duly accomplished early in September with the minimum of "fuss and bother" in the face of a singularly inactive enemy, who on the left of our bridgehead even allowed a road net to be installed ahead of the forward movement of our troops. Later in the month, however, any attempt by patrols to press too boldly to the north from our new positions was resisted strongly by the well entrenched enemy guarding the approaches to the great dark massif of Kowang San (355 metres) that rose sharp and clear against the blue of the Korean sky. At times the sudden squalls of hostile mortar and artillery fire reminded one of the sterner contests of the fields of France - a warning and a portent of the future for those who would take the hint.

September, with its crisp dew on russet bracken and greenery, and its sharp tang of the stengthening autumn, began to draw to its close, when suddenly the Commonwealth Division was ordered to take part in a major corps operation called "Commando." The objects were threefold: (1) To clear the enemy away from the railway which runs over the Imjin River and then turns north-eastward towards Chorwon and Kumhwa. The accomplishment of this task would greatly improve the logistical situation by reducing the demands on road transport during the coming winter. (2) To capture certain high ground up to a line called Jamestown, which would make it more difficult for the enemy to mount a large offensive. (3) To inflict the maximum losses.

The 1st Corps Commander Gen. O'Daniel, had little room to manoeuvre or to concentrate his strength, as all his four Divisions were already committed defensively in the forward area. He therefore decided to leave the 1st R.O.K. Division (South Korean) in situ on his left flank, and to make an almost simultaneous straightforward attack with his three other Divisions: (left) 1st Commonwealth Division, (centre) 1st Cavalry Division United States (this is an Infantry Division), and (right) 3rd Infantry Division United States."D" Day was eventually fixed for October 3rd, 1951.

Plans

Our Division's task in the Corps' operation was to capture the dominating features of Maryang San (317 metres), Kowang San (355 metres) and the tangle of smaller hills that run south-west from Point 210 to 187 metres to the south-west. This was no easy task for the Divisional Commander, Maj.-Gen. A. J. H. Cassels. Besides the formidable nature of the ground on which the enemy was disposed in depth and strength, he really had only two infantry Brigades intact for the battle, as the headquarters and units of the 29th Brigade (Brigadier Brodie) were in the process of being relieved by fresh personnel and units from Britain and Hong Kong. The problem was solved, as our story will show, by an adroit and neat shuffle of the cards in his pack and the taking of something of a calculated risk, to mass his strength on the right. The 25th Canadian Brigade (Brigadier Rockingham) holding the right of the Divisional Sector was extended further to the south-west to hold most of the Divisional front, and enough strength was found from the 29th Brigade to hold the extreme left. The latter Brigade was also to provide the 1st Royal Northumberland Fusiliers ready to reinforce at the appropriate moment the 28th Commonwealth Brigade (Brigadier Taylor), which formation was to strike the main blow.

The Divisional Commander's plan to secure the line Jamestown, in a nutshell, was as follows:-

Phase 1: October 3; 28th Commonwealth Brigade. Objective: Area Point 355.
Phase 2: October 4; 25th Canadian Brigade. Objective: Area Point 187.
Phase 3: October 5; 28th Commonwealth Brigade. Objective: Area Point 317.

The full weight of the Divisional artillery, augmented by two batteries of 8 inch howitzers and two batteries of 155 howitzers, and one battery of "Long Toms," over 120 cannon and 4.2 mortars - a respectable total for the Korean War. This fire power was to support each Brigade in turn. The 28th Commonwealth Brigade group consisted of the following units:-

1st Battalion King's Own Scottish Borderers (Lt.-Col. MacDonald).
1st Battalion King's Shropshire Light Infantry (Lt.-Col. Barlow).
3rd Battalion Royal Australian Regiment (Lt.-Col. Hassett).
16th Royal New Zealand Field Regiment (Major Webb).
11th (Sphinx) Light Mortar Battery, R.A.
12th Field Squadron R.E.
60th Indian Field Ambulance.

In addition, the 8th Hussar (Lt.-Col. Sir G. Lowther), less one squadron, were placed in support. The 28th Brigade had been in the field about six months, its casualties had been light and the previous training amongst the hills of Hong Kong had been a great asset to the two British Battalions - now war-hardened and fit. They were "strong trees that would stand in any storm."

The 3rd R.A.R. were Korean veterans of a year's standing, but between losses and the rotation of the men back to Australia, the make-up of the Battalion had altered recently. The experienced veterans had, except for about 200 "all ranks," been replaced by young Regulars. This well-balanced amalgam of experience and freshness, carefully trained and practised in minor operations by the new Commanding Officer, Lt.-Col. Hassett, was soon to prove its mettle. As for the New Zealand Field Regiment, no gunners knew more about how to solve gunnery problems peculiar to Korea, and how to get the shell to the target, quickly and accurately.

For Phase 3, the 1st Battalion Royal Northumberland Fusiliers (Lt.-Col. M. C. Speer) was borrowed from 29th Brigade and placed under my command. This battalion had been hard hit in the Battle of the Imjin and was now keen to get its own back.

The Brigade Plot

When Brigade planning of the operation first started we did not know a great deal about the enemy. With the assistance of the Intelligence Branch at Division and air photographs we managed to cast some strong gleams of light through the prevailing fog of war before "D" Day. The Chinese 65th Army was opposite us on our front (the term Army, however, must not be taken too seriously as it really means a Corps). This Army was disposed with one division forward and two in reserve. It was believed that the 191st Division had recently relieved the 192nd Division. The Regiments (Borderers) in the 191st Division were believed to be deployed two up and one in reserve, one regiment being disposed south of the east-west lateral road and one north-east of it, with the remaining one in reserve. This meant that our four Battalions would strike at the best part of a division, with other reserves handy.

The good and efficient enemy camouflage made it difficult for us, even with the aid of air photographs, to pin-point enemy positions, but working from an analysis of his tactical habits, we were able to locate roughly most of his company's positions. We did, however, have accurate information about Point 199. This feature was only held by an enemy section - a grave tactical error on his part, of which we took every advantage. In fact, by not holding this position strongly he gave us room to manoeuvre and exert leverage.

The Chinese troops opposing us were well equipped as regards small arms and mortars. It was also realised that they had an increased amount of artillery, but we all underestimated the number of guns he really had. The enemy during the summer had completed a strong defensive system of deep bunkers and trenches in considerable depth. The Bridge plan for the early stages of the 1st phase amounted to two straight left punches, delivered by the 1st King's Shropshire Light Infantry and 1st King's Own Scottish Borderers directed at Points 210 and 355 respectively. After Point 210 had been captured the King's Shropshire Light Infantry were to exploit to Point 227. The 3rd R.A.R. were to deliver a right hook, with elements of the Battalion to seize Point 199, with the dual purpose of exerting pressure against the rear slopes of Kowang San (355 metres) and to obtain a springboard for Phase 3.

The King's Shropshire Light Infantry planned as a first step to capture Point 208 by a Company night operation by 06.00 hours. This feature was believed to be held by a weak outpost. This would help to secure the left flank of the Brigade attack and give the Battalion a flying start for its next step. On the capture of Point 210, 2,000 yards to the west, the King's Shropshire Light Infantry were then to swing north-west and exploit to Point 227. The purposes of this move were as follows:-

(a) It would bring the Battalion into its final defensive position on the western slopes of Kowang San, which I had decided to hold in strength, as a penetration here would endanger the whole Brigade.

(b) The Canadian Brigade, on the completion of Phase 2, by a sidestep to the right were to extend their boundary to the east-west road.
(c) The capture of Point 227 would bring about a partial envelopment of Kowang San and in addition, if the King's Shropshire Light Infantry operation went quickly, they would be able to hold the ring, whilst the King's Own Scottish Borderers dealt with Kowang San (Point 355).

With the only good road in the area fit for tanks the Light Infantry men were allotted for support one squadron 8th Hussars (Major de Clermont). From 05.45 to 07.00 hour the full weight of the artillery was placed in support to give them a good start. At the latter hour the bulk of the artillery was to be switched to the support of the 1st King's Own Scottish Borderers, leaving one Regiment for the support of the King's Shropshire Light Infantry. A troop of Engineers from 12th Field Squadron was allotted to the Battalion to open the east-west road.

The 1st King's Own Scottish Borderers had the onerous task of capturing Kowang San (Point 355). The Battalion planned to attack on a two-Company front plus the battle patrol. The main thrust was to be directed at Long and Kidney Ridge and thence due west to envelop the western shoulders of Point 355, thus avoiding the steep cliff-like approach from the south-east. This conception fitted in admirably with the Brigade plan.

The task of the right-hand Company 'B' (Major Harrison), was to seize the Finger and thus protect the flank of the main effort, opening the way for a subsequent advance on to the north-western shoulder of Point 355. Thus it was hoped that Point 355 would fall to a double envelopment aided by fire into its reverse slopes from Point 199. Fire support consisted of two Field Regiments, one battery 4.2 mortars and the Corps artillery allotted to the Division. After the initial timed concentrations, the more flexible and economical method of concentrations "on call" were to be used.

The 4.2 mortars were to "blanket off" the top of Point 355 with smoke and the machine-gunners of the King's Shropshire Light Infantry had the task of neutralising part of this feature. The King's Own Scottish Borderers were to move on D-I unobserved into an assembly position in the area of Point 238 and Korung just behind the covering patrols of the Vandoos, 2nd Battalion Royal 22e Canadian Regiment. It was decided to filter the leading Companies into position in daylight by moving over the rough scrub-covered ground 75 yards between men.

Two Companies of the 3rd R.A.R. were also to filter forward at the same time, to an assembly area just north and east of Point 238. In the early hours of the morning of "D" Day, under the cover of darkness, 'B' Company (Major Nicholls) was then to carry out a silent night attack on to Point 199. As soon as this was captured "A" Company, with a couple of sections of machine-guns, were to move up to support them and the tanks of the half-squadron would follow at first light to carry out with the machine-gun sections there fire role of hitting at the rear of Point 355. The balance of the 3rd R.A.R. were to remain in Brigade reserve with a half squadron 8th Hussars.

The overall Brigade fire plan consisted of U concentrations from 05.00 hours to 05.45 hours on all known enemy artillery and mortar positions and M concentrations on all suspected positions of the same type. Worked in with this programme were a series of brief concentrations on infantry localities in depth to "soften them up."

Aided by artificial moonlight, our Engineers worked manfully for two nights before the attack, under the very noses of the enemy, to drive a road north of hills which lie between Points 183 and 238.

The Battle of Kowang San and Maryang San

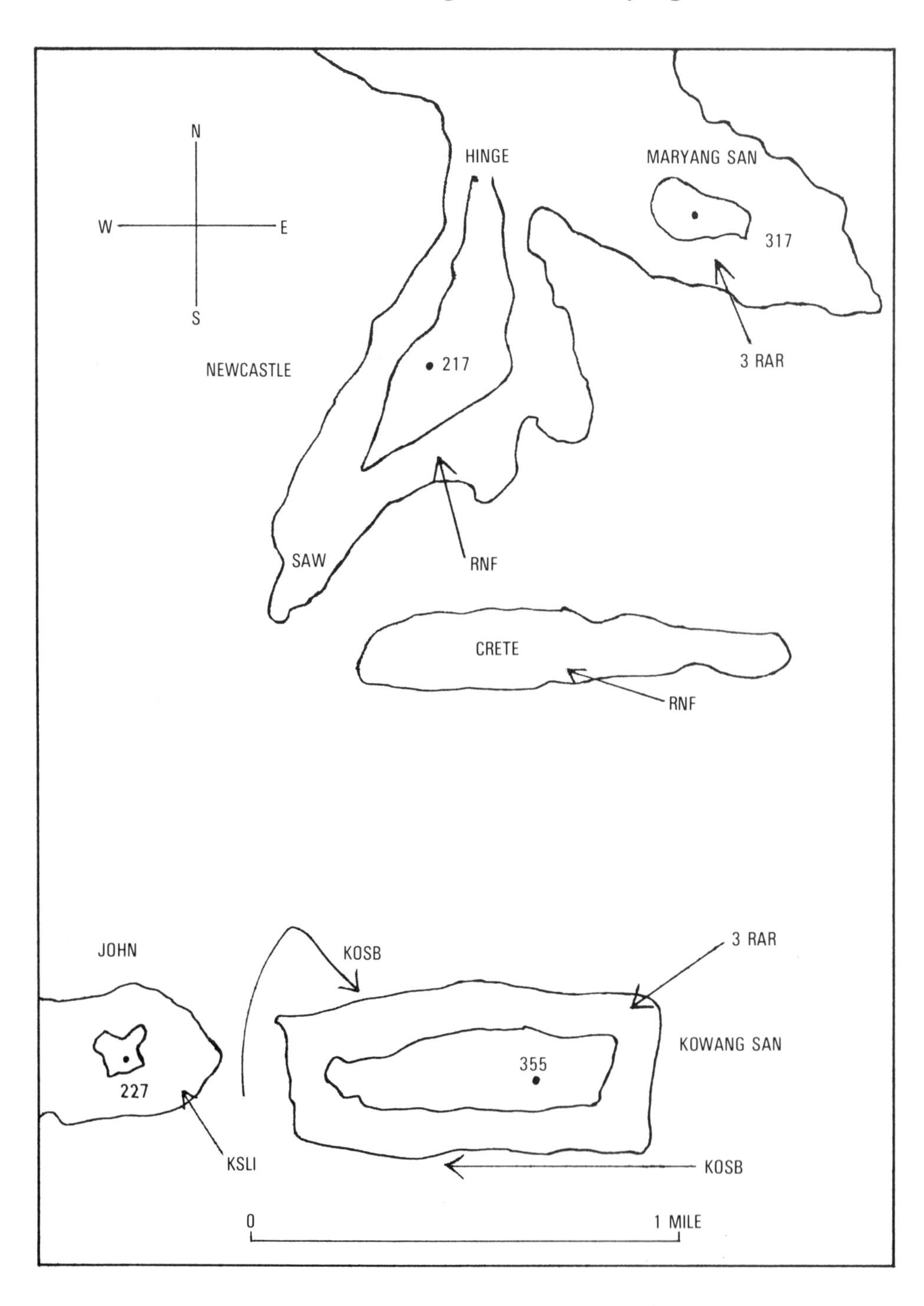

Meanwhile, the bulk of the Brigade was moving secretly to its concentration area (see sketch) and thence Battalions moved forward to their different assembly areas. By D-I, undetected by the enemy, six rifle companies (King's Own Scottish Borderers and 3rd R.A.R.) lay under the hot afternoon sun amongst the scrub and brush on or near Point 238. Further to the south the 1st King's Shropshire Light Infantry had also reached, without interference, their assembly area. Last minute preparations were calmly completed in the forward companies, and now nothing remained but to get, under the silent canopy of heaven, the rest allowed by the situation, the chill of the night air and those feelings known only to fighting men on such occasions.

Part 2 - Into Battle

At 05.00 hours on October 3 over 120 of our guns and mortars suddenly split the darkness with their lightning and rent the earth with their metal. On the left the leading troops of the King's Shropshire Light Infantry, 'D' Company, were by now moving to the end of a night approach, that was almost perfect in its management. Half an hour later they moved up to assault Point 208, now just showing in the false light that comes before the dawn. Their quarry had fled. Quickly the Light Infantry men moved to consolidate on pre-arranged positions; there was some hostile mortaring. The code word was rapidly flashed over the wireless and the rest of the Battalion began to follow up.

Whilst these events had been taking place on the left flank, an equally successful action took place on the right flank. The leading elements of 'B' Company, 3rd R.A.R., left their F.U.P. at 03.00 hours and crept silently down the hillside across the paddy-fields and up the further slopes to Point 199. The night was very dark but the top of the feature was just visible silhouette against the faint silver gleam of the stars. A silent deadly rush and the small enemy post was overwhelmed and a bewildered prisoner hustled to the rear. Soon the second Company ('A') with the machine-gunners moved up on to the hill. At first light a troop of tanks of 8th Hussars, having moved up the rough road constructed by the Royal Engineers, went down the hill and safely negotiated the soft "paddy" and with engines roaring and tracks clattering moved up the ridge to Point 199 to join the infantry.

An important door of the defence had been forced. The enemy should have locked and bolted it more securely. The Australians and the 8th Hussars were now in a position to influence the battle for Kowang San (Point 355) from the rear.

Daylight

Just before 07.00 hours the two leading Companies of the 1st King's Own Scottish Borderers, 'C' Company (Major Little) left and 'B' Company (Major Harrison) right, got out of their shell scrapes and slit trenches and moved forward to the attack. Our artillery was now blasting "Long Ridge" and "Finger Ridge" and the Borderers' machine-gunners were aiding them with a continous sheet of fire. The top of Kowang San was, after a weak start, now shrouded in thick white smoke and the silver and gold bursts of phosphorus mortar bombs could be seen continuously arriving to stir up this witch's cauldron. The effectiveness of the screen was proved by the following wireless intercept from the Chinese O.P. on the top of Point 355: "I cannot see anything. All my signallers and mortar men are dead," then silence.

On the left the efforts of the squadron of Centurions to join up with the forward troops of the King's Shropshire Light Infantry were proving abortive. Quaking paddy-fields, scattered mines and the rugged ravine slotted hills imposed commonsense caution on these great steel monsters. This placed the Commanding

Officer of King's Shropshire Light Infantry in something of a dilemma for he had counted heavily on the support of the tanks to speed his advance and to cut down the casualties in his rifle companies. After some delay the Battalion moved forward without the bulk of its supporting armour. Major Taite's 'B' Company, turning in a south-westerly direction, neatly drove the enemy off a small eminence, which enfiladed the main line of advance. On the whole, however, progress was slow against spasmodic resistance from enemy covering troops, and the end of the day found the Battalion about one thousand yards east of the strongly held Point 210.

In the centre, 'B' Company, King's Own Scottish Borderers, had secured the "Finger" spur north of "Long Ridge" without much difficulty, but on "Long Ridge" itself a bitter struggle had flared up and went on for about three hours. An enemy company was entrenched in well-sighted and ingeniously dug positions. He fought with great tenacity and had to be rooted out of each position in turn. The enemy concealed on the thick eastern slopes of this 600 yards long feature had not been properly mopped up and soon snipers had isolated the attacking 'C' Company and began to fire into their rear. The situation became confused and Major Little decided to pull his Company back to the eastern edge of the hill, reorganise and with a fresh fire plan, go in again. The Company withdrew covered by one of its rifle platoons.

About 12.00 hours the news of this setback came over the wireless to me at Point 238. The report was that the Company had been counter-attacked. This was the vital point of the battle and I therefore moved off my perch on Point 238 towards the King's Own Scottish Borderers, and after waiting a little while in the narrow gully to let things simmer, climbed up the track on the hillside. On arrival at the Colonel's command post I felt my journey had hardly been necessary as John MacDonald had the situation well in hand. He had bolstered up 'C' Company's right with elements of 'B' Company from the north and brought forward 'A' Company from his reserve and was about to put in a combined attack under Major Duncan with both 'A' and 'C' Companies. In the early afternoon this fresh attack went in covered with a strong artillery and mortar concentration, the fire of machine-guns, and last but not least, the skirl of a lone piper. This time there was no mistake about it and a close-quarter battle ended decisively in favour of the Scots at 15.30 hours, giving the enemy no time to collect himself. 'A' Company moved down from "Long Ridge" and went for the "Kidney Ridge" feature, and after a tough little action secured it. Time now for mountain-wise soldiers to stand fast and to reorganise to meet the tests of darkness.

The complicated processes of consolidation were carried forward long into the night, combined with preparations to storm points 210, 227 and 355 as early as possible next morning. Commanders, staff officers, signallers, sappers, riflemen, gunners , drivers and porters all played their part. A short telephone conversation between the Divisional Commander and myself quickly settled the question of artillery support. I asked for the bulk of the artillery up till 10.00 hours - the General wisely gave us an extra hour; that is, up to 11.00 hours - which proved just right. The 25th Canadian Brigade attack was put back a few hours to 11.00 hours.

I decided to use part of my reserve in tomorrow's battle and ordered the 3rd R.A.R. to attack Wangjing Myon, just north-east of Point 355, with one company to exert the maximum pressure and to make certain of a double envelopment.

4th October

Shortly before dawn the continuous rapid thud-thud of our artillery could be heard giving the strongly held Point 210 feature an intense concentration of fire to ease the path of the King's Shropshire Light Infantry. During the night Lt.-Col. Barlow had brought forward his reserve 'D' Company (Major Cottle) from Point 208 and backed it with elements of 'C' Company (Capt. Houghton-Berry).

The assault company was joined by the three tanks of the 8th Hussars, the winners and sole survivors of a squadron steeplechase drive over thickly covered rock and ridge. Strangely enough, they were all subalterns and the Troop Commanders thereby proving, as one wit put it, "the advantages of a superior education." The enemy resisted strongly and there was heavy and close fighting before the stormers could carry the position. But in the end, well handled by Major Cottle, nothing could stop the determined and well-trained Light Infantry men and the three magnificent tank crews. Outshot and outfought, the brave Chinese defensive was swept aside and Point 210 was secured at 10.00 hours. Numerous enemy dead littered bunkers and trenches. The Commanding Officer, Lt.-Col. Barlow, then ordered 'A' Company (Major Heard) to move north-west to exploit Point 227. Whilst the fight had run like a flame over Point 210, a section of the 12th Field Squadron, under the command of Capt. Pollard, Royal Engineers, had boldly prodded their way up the east-west road under shell fire, a troop of tanks working up the road behind them. This armour was now nicely placed to support 'A' Company's attack on Point 227, which was finally cleared just before dark in the face of mortar, bazooka and small arms fire, the latter delivered at short range.

Whilst the King's Shropshire Light Infantry were battling for Point 210, the King's Own Scottish Borderers Company (Major Robertson MacLeod) and the Battle Platoon had kept abreast of them and on the fall of Point 210 they moved boldly and rapidly around and up the western slopes of Kowang San and stormed the top covered by artillery and machine-gun fire. By 11.00 hours the crest of the feature was in our hands. The enemy garrison did not offer much resistance from the top of this massive ridge and Robertson MacLeod's men soon had them running for their lives down the northern slopes. As the Scots were moving up to assault from the west, 'D' Company (Major Girke), 3rd R.A.R. were about to assault the Wangjing Myon feature. There was a sharp and bloody struggle at close quarters and the enemy were driven helter-skelter from this important position. At the same time 'B' Company, King's Own Scottish Borderers, to the south of the Australians, were exerting pressure against the east shoulder of Kowang San. Thus hard fighting and skilled manoeuvre had led to a double envelopment of this strong commanding feature, and this, combined with the fire of the tanks and machine-guns from the Point 199 feature, had brought about its capture with under 100 casualties in all three battalions - a tribute to the skill and determination of the infantry and to the peerless support of Hussars, gunners and sappers. The 25th Canadian Brigade were now able to implement Phase 2 against the long Point 187 feature unhindered by enemy observation from the north. By the end of the day, after a quick and spirited advance, they had almost completed their contract.

Phase 3 October 5

During the afternoon, whilst the captured ground was being consolidated, the finishing touches were being put to the plan for Phase 3. Briefly, the Brigade plan called for a pincer movement: one battalion 1st Royal Northumberland Fusiliers and to move on the axis of the narrow valley that runs to the west just north of Wangjing Myon and thence on to and up the Point 217 feature and finally to capture a ring contour called the "Hinge", which lay about 1,000 yards to the north-east of Point 217. The other battalion, 3rd R.A.R., was to sweep along the high ground north of the valley on to the Point 317 ridge and join up with the Fusiliers on the "Hinge". Both attacks were to start at 05.45 hours (first light). A fine fire plan of the same type as for 'D' Day was laid on, which included counter-battery and counter-mortar shoots. The top of Point 317 was to be smoked off by 4.2 mortar fire. Covering fire for the assaulting infantry was allotted as follows:

1st Royal Northumberland Fusiliers: One field regiment; one 4.2 battery; machine-guns of King's Own Scottish Borderers and King's Shropshire Light Infantry; tank fire from Point 238.

3rd Royal Australian Regiment: Two field regiments; half squadron tanks. Air strikes were to be placed in depth on most of the high ground on an arc north and west of the final objectives.

The reader will realise that, as tomorrow would be the third day of the offensive, the Chinese would have had ample time to alert and move reserves and get set to meet our onslaught. Already fierce and bloody fighting was taking place on our right on the front of the 1st Cavalry Division. As if to compensate the attacking troops, Providence that morning threw in a makeweight, for as dawn broke a veil of thick mist shrouded the arena. A little later on in the morning Maryang San (317 metres) could be seen with its base wreathed in a white fog and its bare steep top clear and sharp against a bright yellow sun, which had swept the heavens clear.

The two battalions made good use of this friendly cloak. On the left, down the valley, the Fusiliers pressed on rapidly with two companies forward. At about 10.00 hours 'Y' Company had reached the western end of "Crete" and 'Z' Company a point 500 yards east of Point 217. Then both companies halted to orient themselves and to let the mist clear. About an hour later the visibility improved and "Y" Company pushed on and occupied "Saw", and a little later 'Z' Company reached the top of the Point 217 feature, surprising the enemy, killing some and taking 10 prisoners. But the enemy quickly recovered from his surprise and attempts to clear the shole ridge were frustrated by a most determined, numerous and well-entrenched enemy. As the Fusiliers probed for soft spots they were met with withering fire and then small-scale counter-attacks delivered with showers of hand grenades. They were hard put to it to hold their ground and troubled by the rapid rate at which they had to use up their small arms ammunition and, to add to their difficulties, the wireless sets chose in this area that day to be somewhat erratic. Nevertheless, they fought on with the tenacity of the "Fighting Fifth" and all attempts to shift them from their toehold were beaten off.

Meanwhile, the Australian battalion had also got to grips with the enemy. In the mist they had obtained a footing on the ridge, to the north of their springboard at Point 199, and swinging west, 'D' Company (Major Hardiman) moved through the leading company and pushed steadily in the direction of Point 317. On nearing a triangle of three rounded sandstone bumps which rise above the general level of the ridge, they heard the enemy throwing hand-grenades nervously, then suddenly the zing of enemy rifle bullets and out of the thinning mist the Company, like a cloudburst, fell on the enemy. Most of the Chinese machine-guns and light automatics were facing south as the attack came in from the east; in and over, down and along the trenches with bursts of bren, rattling Owen guns, and blast of hand-grenades they swept. Nothing could stop this dashing attack. It was soon over and a strong company position had fallen.

The mist having disappeared, Lt. Smith, who had taken over the command from the wounded Major Hardiman, organised the Company for its next step, which was the capture of the Company locality a few hundred yards to the west, which barred the final approach to the top of Maryang San. If the last action was a fine example of a coup de main in war, the next was to be an equally splendid action, in which those three arms of the Services - infantry, artillery and armour - all worked in harmony to the speedy and inevitable destruction of the enemy.

"H" hour was fixed for 14.00 hours and the Commanding Officer, Lt.-Col. Hassett, also brought into play 'A' Company, who were to attack west along the Point 199 ridge towards Point 317, thus aiding the main thrust. Promptly on the down came the fire of two field regiments on the enemy trenches, which seamed and creviced 'D' Company's objective - ugly dun-coloured bursts of 3-in. mortar fire, thickening up the rear of this concentration of flying steel and explosive. The infantry worked their way up to within 200 yards of the cowering enemy and then the artillery lifted - and in they went swiftly with the bayonet and grenade, covered by the carefully controlled, precise and devastating fire of Major Butler's Centurions. Grimly the infantrymen made short work of the defenders and another bastion of the defence had gone. 'A' Company, to the immediate south, though they could not make much ground, had pinned down the enemy opposite them and prevented them interfering with 'D' Company.

Point 317 Falls

Keeping the forward impetus of his battalion going, the Commanding Officer leapfrogged 'C' Company (Major Girke) through on his main thrust line and, covered by artillery and tank fire, the Australian Infantrymen climbed the dusty steep and narrow slopes of pinnacle-shaped Point 317, in some places climbing on all fours, and in the late afternoon secured it in the face of spasmodic fire before the enemy could reinforce this vital point. The 3rd R.A.R. had, by their resolute, rapid and skilled attack, sheared their way through a strong defensive position. At Point 217 a battle was still raging and the intensity of enemy counter-attacks, coming up and through the cover of the wooden western slopes, had increased. The Fusiliers were down to their last few rounds and in 'Z' Company two platoons had lost half their strength. The decision was taken to withdraw them to "Crete". Having first of all evacuated their wounded, the North Country men dourly fell back, covered by the fire of our artillery. Their bold morning thrust and hard afternoon fight had undoubtedly absorbed enemy reinforcements now arriving in strength, and thus the Fusiliers contributed in no mean measure to the success of their neighbours on the more important ground to the north-east.

Counter-attacks

A plan was now made for October 6 for 1st Royal Northumberland Fusiliers, who had two fresh rifle companies in hand, to put in a converging attack on to the stubborn and strongly held Point 217 feature. One rifle company was to move through Point 317 and along the ridge to the "Hinge", whilst the rest of the Battalion returned to the attack on the old axis, but making the actual assault along the ridge in a north-easterly direction instead of from east to west as on the previous day. During the night, however, the idea of moving a company through the Australians was reluctantly given up because of the long and difficult night climb before the troops could get to their start line, and also to lesser extent, the difficulty of supplying them away from the Battalion. Instead the 3rd R.A.R. were asked to help by vigorous probing and the use of fire power from Point 317. On October 6, under cover of an early morning mist, a fighting patrol of the 3rd R.A.R. surprised the enemy on a small feature 400 yards to the west of Point 317; this position was promptly secured and, with the aid of artillery, held against a couple of small counter-attacks. The 1st Royal Northumberland Fusiliers attacked at 10.50 hours after 'Y' Company had first of all secured a "firm base" on "Saw" in the face of the artillery and erratic small arms fire. The assault company, 'W,' dealt with some scattered opposition when moving through the thick country up the ridge and reached the edge of their objective, but efforts to push forward were stopped by the close fire of four machine-guns, two of which were positioned in or near a bunker.

Flanking movements were tried first to the right up the steep eastern face, but this was stopped by showers of grenades, then a movement to the left in the thick country, which ended in a stalemate, as the enemy was holding the wooden western slopes in strength. Hostile mortar and artillery fire increased and losses began to mount, particularly in officers. "X" Company was brought into action and advanced, using phosphorus grenades, but they could not break the deadlock. The Australians, on high ground, were doing their best to help by firing into the enemy's rear and the King's Shropshire Light Infantry machine-guns were trying to stop the flow of enemy reinforcements from the west. Several enemy counter-attacks were beaten off. In the late afternoon, in the face of a massing enemy and a movement to cut in behind the two companies, permission was given for withdrawal at discretion. Later on, in the face of a strong counter-attack coming in from the north and west, the Fusiliers withdrew skilfully covered by "Y" Company from the firm base.

The strong resistance offered by the enemy on this ridge may seem somewhat illogical, as we already held the dominating ground at Points 355 and 317, but it would seem that the Chinese had not given up the hope of retaking Point 317, and it also was very probable that he thought we were going to try and push out much further to the west beyond the line Jamestown.

I decided to make no further effort with the 1st Royal Northumberland Fusiliers, but to edge forward gradually from the high ground on the north and to try and subdue the enemy on the Point 217 ridge, with continuous air strikes, artillery and mortar fire by day and strong harassing fire at night to isolate and wear out the garrison. As a first step the 3rd R.A.R. were to seize the "Hinge", which was about 300 yards away from their foremost positions. They were then to push patrols south-west. The "Hinge" was duly secured, but the infantry had greater difficulty in consolidating their gains in the face of very heavy shell fire, a great deal of which was a heavy calibre. All that day there was a continuous succession of air strikes and artillery bombardments of the Point 217 area, scorching and sapping the vegetation and the spirit of the enemy. Our gunners were also striving to knock out the enemy artillery, the General bringing into play some of the Corps artillery. Our air O.P.s did some gallant and skilful work locating the hostile batteries. In the afternoon a serious situation arose because the very heavy shelling disorganised the porter trains of the 3rd R.A.R. moving on Point 317 and the fighting troops were already short of ammunition. Therefore a decision had to be taken to strip the King's Own Scottish Borderers and King's Shropshire Light Infantry of a proportion of their porters to help the Australians. The Royal Engineers also gave generous help to meet this emergency. The Battalion was successfully resupplied before nightfall. It was just as well, for early in the night the enemy counter-attacked in strength against our localities lying along the ridge just to the west of Point 317. This attack was well supported by artillery fire, which included S.P. guns firing at close range. The Divisional artillery, which was brought into action with speed, played a great part in smashing up this attack decisively, and the machine-guns of the King's Shropshire Light Infantry were also used with effect. The Australians, with humanity, let the Chinese stretcher bearers remove the wounded, who in many cases lay quite close to the defenders' trenches. For days afterwards the putrid stench of dead bodies poisoned the air.

On the morning of the 27th steps had already been taken to bring about the relief of the hard tried 3rd R.A.R. who had fought throughout with such dash and tenacity, and early the next morning the King's Own Scottish Borderers began steadily to take over the Point 317 area. A little later in the day, after some very gallant and effective air strikes by the South African Mustang Squadron, it was sensed that the enemy had accepted the logic of the situation and had withdrawn off the battle-scarred ridge. Patrols confirmed this and before nightfall the 1st Royal Northumberland Fusiliers and the 1st King's Own Scottish Borderers had moved up companies and occupied Point 217.

Thus ended this hard-fought action. The cost in life and limb was fairly light, Divisional casualties being 420, of which 28th Brigade suffered the bulk; 100 prisoners were taken and at least 1,000 of the enemy killed.

On 9th October 1951, Major-General A. J. H. Cassels, CB, CBE, DSO, received this message from Major-General J. W. O'Daniel, the Commander of the U.S. 1st Corps:

"I want to express to you my admiration for the way in which the 1st British Commonwealth Division attacked and seized its objectives during Operation Commando. It was a masterful manoeuvre skilfully combining aggressiveness and complete, detailed planning, resulting in the taking of key terrain features with a minimum cost in manpower and with full exploitation of available fire power.

The attainment of your objectives has secured critical terrain, dominating avenues of approach successfully utilised by the enemy in past counter offensives and denies to him the use of important assembly areas for future attacks against our forces. Your operation was conducted in a manner fully in keeping with the finest traditions of the military service and is a tribute to the courage and professional skill of your officers and men."

Chapter 4

THE HOOK

By General Sir George Cooper GCB, MC

The Hook was the scene of fierce defensive battles by the Black Watch and the Duke of Wellington's Regiment in 1952 and 1953. The Hook was a hill feature jutting forward on the left of the 1st Commonwealth Division's front, some 8 miles north of the River Imjin. The Division faced Chinese Communist forces who were dug in on the hills to the north of anything up to 2 miles away. Their positions converged in the vicinity of the Hook and the forward lefthand platoon was dug in less than 100 yds. away. The feature was some 150 yds. broad and 300 yds. deep, sufficient for only a company, but if the enemy had gained possession of it they would have been able to overlook not only the flanking position but also all the rear areas right back to the Imjin River. A withdrawal would have been inevitable, not only for the Division but probably for the whole of I Corps, and the nearest tenable defence line to the south would have been beyond the river in the general area of Gloster Hill, the scene of such fierce fighting some two years earlier. It was thus imperative that 1st Commonwealth Division should hold the Hook and it rightly qualified for the term "vital ground".

The defence of the Hook was made especially difficult and dangerous by the big increase in Chinese artillery fire during the static war. When the Black Watch took over the Hook from the US Marines in November 1952, the Commanding Officer asked 55 Field Squadron Royal Engineers to turn it into a fortress by constructing really strong bunkers, deep communication trenches, tunnels and chambers in which troops could rest in comparative safety and shelter during heavy bombardments. This work was in progress when the Black Watch fought a bloody battle to hold it.

Early in the New Year, the Division was placed in reserve and it was not until April 1953, when the thaw had set in, that the Division returned to its old positions. As a result of continuous shelling and mortaring, the forward trench linking up the various weapon pits was virtually untenable. In place of the deep, sandbagged trench along the forward slope was a wide and shallow "V", along which it was impossible to move in daylight without attracting enemy attention. There was no other cover, the scrub and bushes having all disappeared in the shelling until the hill looked like a World War 1 scene. It was a thoroughly unhealthy place.

The position was once more held by the Black Watch with 1 Troop of 55 Field Squadron in support. The Troop's first task was to deepen the forward trench and convert it into a covered way, connecting up the various weapon pits. It was a daunting prospect, as the enemy could see what was going on and work was mainly confined to the hours of darkness. Progress could be seen at daybreak and mortaring and shelling were constant as soon as work started.

With so little room to dig positions, the company had two platoons forward and one in depth 150 yds further back, just behind the top of the hill. The forward left-handed platoon had a good field of fire towards the closest Chinese positions along a connected saddle to a pimple of ground nicknamed "Ronson". A dug-in flame-thrower was available to assist them at the nearest position to the enemy.

The forward right-hand platoon had a good field of fire along a bare ridge to its north-east and patrols could sneak out this way by night. To its immediate front, though, was a small spur called "Green Finger" with such convex slopes that it was possible for the enemy to form up unseen and launch a surprise attack. To overcome this problem it was decided to build a tunnel down the spur and to break out either side of the ridge with a machine gun bunker which could fire down the slope. The start of the tunnel was from the corner of the forward trench.

By April/May 1953, construction of the tunnel and the forward covered trench was well advanced. Shelling and mortaring were fairly continuous and all work was being carried out by night. Every vestige of cover had long since disappeared and the ground was littered with all the debris of war: tangled barbed wire, bent pickets, shattered timber, torn sandbags, scattered ammunition, enemy stick grenades and the odd dead Chinaman stuck in the wire. The individual section posts provided less and less protection for their inhabitants and it was decided to build really strong bunkers with embrasures of reinforced concrete which could stand up to the increasing weight of enemy firepower. These bunkers were dug out of the side of the forward trench, lined with heavy baulks of timber and with interlocking concrete lintels at the front, the whole covered with 3 to 4 ft of earth and rocks. These lintels, each weighing 600-800 lb, were constructed in the Field Park and had to be dragged over the top of the Hook, through the shell craters and debris, and into their forward positions. This could only be done on the darkest of nights and the local Korean labourers displayed great courage in carrying out this hazardous work. It is not always easy to teach a Korean that the safest thing to do when a flare lights up the surrounding area is to "freeze" - there is an almost overwhelming desire to run! With the enemy so close, this feeling was not entirely confined to the Koreans.

Some 40yds back from the forward position was the gunner OP, dug in on the brow of the hill with the forward platoon HQ, which co-ordiated both forward platoons, immediately behind it. By the night the Forward Observation Officer moved back to Company HQ on the reserve slope. All positions were connected by deep, World War 1 type, communication trenches and repair work on them was a continuous night time task for the infantry, along with the repair of wires and constant patrolling. By day, most people slept in bunkers or tunnels burrowed into the sides of the hill. After ten days or a fortnight, the company would be relieved and move into reserve for a much needed bath and rest, or on to a neighbouring, quieter position. The Sapper Troop remained, plucking up its courage each evening at dusk for the nightly tasks ahead. The comparative security of the Troop rest area three miles to the rear made the daily journey forward seem all the more nerve-racking.

There were of course many nights when things were quiet and almost peaceful. The enemy would even broadcast from loudspeakers with messages promising freedom from the Yankee yoke for those who surrendered, interspersed with the latest Bing Crosby records. Packets of tea, with a white china peace-dove pinned on top and enclosing a message to "Have a good cup of char and forget the hellish war" would be left for our patrols to find. This form of propaganda had no effect whatsoever on the British soldier - indeed, many wore the peace dove as a cap-badge in their balaclava helmet to show that they had been at the "sharp end"! By day there would be frequent showers of propaganda leaflets and a wild rush to pick up souvenirs would ensue. The only danger to our troops' morale came from the empty mortar canister which made the most terrifying screech as it whirled down to earth ahead of floating leaflets!

The nights were nevertheless always busy and work would be either helped or hindered, depending on one's degree of protection, by the constant stream of flares,

Warsaw Ridge

Views towards Chinese positions from 1 Bn The King's Regiment on the Hook.

usually coming from the American "flare ships" flying overhead. There were also numerous interruptions from sporadic shelling, enemy movement in the vicinity and of course sudden fire-fights. Occasionally, heavier fighting broke out, usually preceeded by heavy shelling for several hours. One such occasion on 7/8 May 1953 presaged a two company size raid on the forward platoons; within five minutes of the attack starting, the platoon commander and the platoon sergeant of the right-hand platoon had been killed and the platoon commander of the left-hand platoon had been mortally wounded. With no news coming to Company HQ the second in command went forward to find out what was happening but in the confusion he could not get anywhere where he could influence the battle. Things looked bleak and the company commander called for reinforcements as well as increasing artillery support. Being of such vital concern to hold the hill, the whole Corps artillery was thrown in, an exciting occasion for the FOO to be calling for an "Uncle" target. Eventually VT fire was brought down to clear the enemy, with terrifying results as all could see when dawn broke and reserve troops had swept the area clear of Chinese.

Limited armoured support was also available but was not always welcomed. Once targets had been spotted, usually by day, on the opposing hills, a Centurion tank would creep up to the crest and fire two or three rounds before retiring behind the hill and closing down against the inevitable enemy reaction. Unfortunately they rarely seemed to think about lesser mortals going about their normal routine and enemy retribution resulted in frantic dives for cover and interrupted tasks. Tanks were not popular. By night, tanks tended to operate in pairs, one with a searchlight to illuminate targets and the other to fire at them.

By the middle of May 1953, the enemy had evidently decided it was time to make another all-out onslaught on the Hook. Shelling increased in intensity, heavier calibre weapons were brought up, with delayed action fuses resulting in deeper penetration of the overhead cover. In a week prior to this major attack 20,000 rounds landed on the position, half of them on the last day, and all of them on a position only 300 yds by 150! Simple mathematics shows that on average one round will fall on about every 2 sq yds but in practice the shape of the ground and the

A panorama from the Hook taken on 19th June 1953 by Padre L. U. Pedersen of NORMASH. Compare with the map on pages 38 and 39.

enemy's endeavours to hit vital strongpoints which had been carefully ranged in during the preceding weeks, made the hits, and hence the damage done, even greater in some places than others. 1 Troop of 55 Field Squadron worked frantically throughout this period to maintain and strengthen the defences.

In the ensuing attack, the Hook, now held by the Duke of Wellington's Regiment, was nearly over-run by sheer weight of numbers and the devastating shelling. Enemy satchel bombs and incendiaries helped to destroy what few defences were left after the last day's terrible bombardment but they were eventually driven off after fierce hand to hand fighting and the tremendous United Nations forces counter bombardment. At first light two Troops of 55 Field Squadron went into the forward company positions to restore some semblance of fire positions for the infantry. Every open trench or weapon pit had been filled in until it was only a scoop in the ground, littered with debris and tangled wire. As a defensive position it had almost ceased to exist and every move forward across the open slopes was accompanied by immediate mortar fire; indeed so close were the enemy that their 60mm mortar bombs could be heard leaving the barrel. Nevertheless, by nightfall sufficient bunkers and weapon pits had been cleared to enable infantry to hold this vital feature and the enemy were fortunately reluctant to renew the contest for a while.

In the last two months of the war, the Hook was held firmly in our hands by the Royal Fusiliers, the King's Regiment and 2 Bn Royal Australian Regiment. Although by the terms of the Armistice Agreement of July 1953 it came into the demilitarised zone, the successful defence kept the southern boundary of the zone north of the Imjin River, leaving the Kansas line intact.

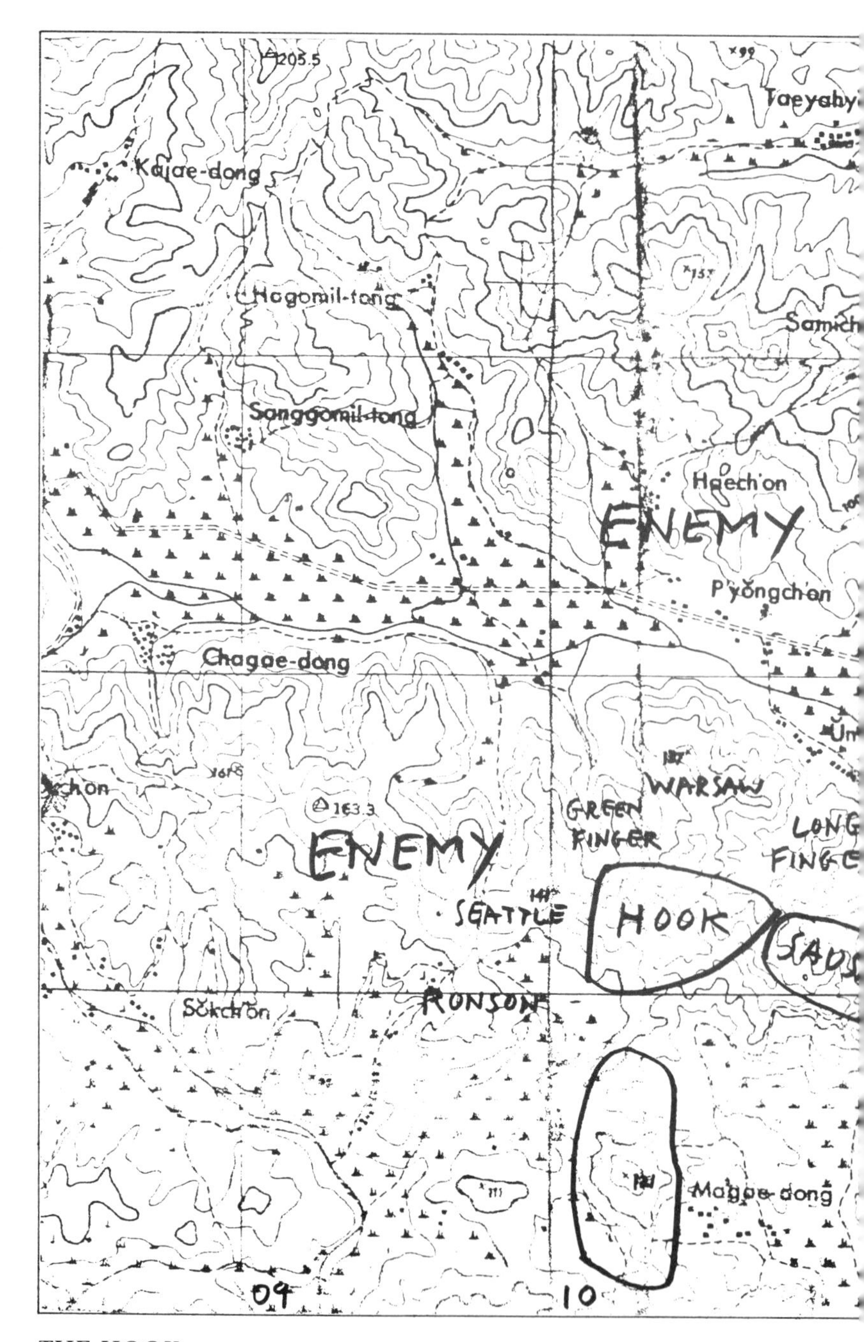
205.5
Kajae-dong
Taeyahy
Hagomil-tong
Samich
Sanggomil-tong
Haech'on
ENEMY
P'yongch'on
Chagae-dong
WARSAW
163.3
GREEN FINGER
LONG FINGE
ENEMY
SEATTLE
HOOK
RONSON
Sokch'on
Magoe-dong
09
10

THE HOOK.

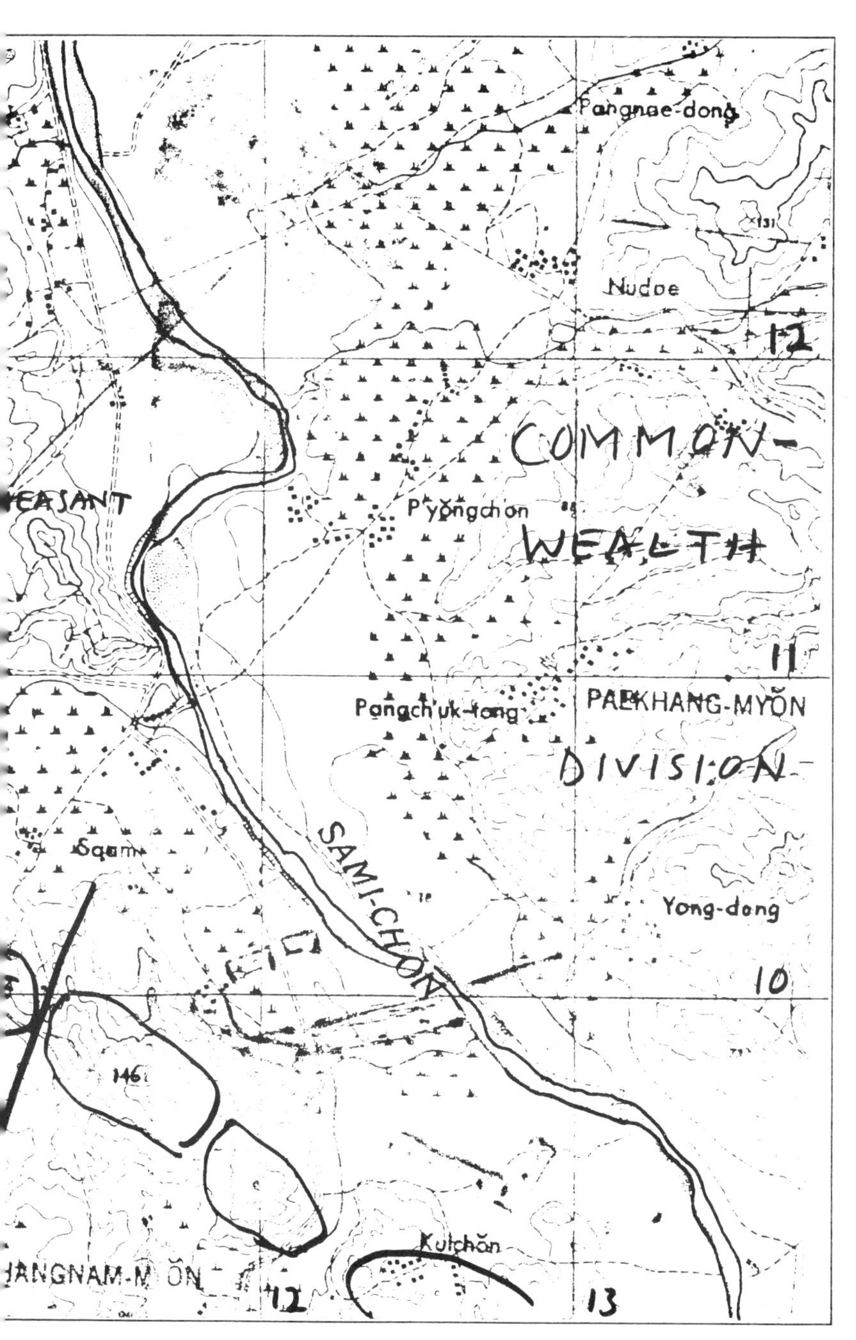

Part of Sheet 6528 11 SW. 2⅝ inches equals about 1 mile. The reason for the Hook's name can be seen from the positions of the two battalions which held it. The horseshoe marking by the Samichon was made by a soldier of DWR in 1953. It was probably a defensive position.

L. U. Pedersen
Looking from the Hook over the entire Commonwealth Division sector as far as 355 in the distance.

L. U. Pedersen
Deep trench on the Hook.

L. U. Pedersen

On the Hook, 19th June 1953. Lieutenant Bob Snell, The King's Regt. and a NORMASH visitor.

L. U. Pedersen

Mills hand grenades placed in the trench wall.

Chapter 5

THE ROYAL NAVY

Adapted by the editors from a series of articles in the Journal of the Royal United Service Institution in 1951-53.

The West Coast Blockade

When hostilities began on 25th June 1950 HM Ships under the command of Rear-Admiral W. G. Andrewes, Flag Officer Second-in-command Far East Station, were dispersed in Japanese waters on a cruise. Under the direction of the Commander-in-Chief, Far East Station, Admiral Sir Patrick Brind, Rear-Admiral Andrewes concentrated his available forces and offered them to the United States authorities for humanitarian purposes. Then, on 29th June, His Majesty's Government placed our ships at the disposal of the Commander, United States Naval Forces, Far East.

At this time, there were 22 British warships in Far East waters. Their duties were widespread, and included the Malayan patrol, the defence of Hong Kong and the Yangtse estuary patrol. Dispositions had to be made quickly, and by reducing other requirements to a minimum, it was possible to put a high percentage of the fleet at the disposal of the Commander United States Naval Forces. By 30th June, the first British ships, which included the light fleet carrier *Triumph*, the cruisers *Belfast* and *Jamaica*, the destroyers *Cossack* and *Consort*, the frigates *Black Swan, Alacrity* and *Hart* and several auxiliaries, had started work with the United States Navy, and it was with pride that at this time our forces on the spot were numerically about as strong as those of the United States Navy. Although over 1,000 miles from the nearest British Base, our ships were logistically self-supporting. From the outset they played a most active and prominent part in establishing that complete naval supremacy so essential to the conduct of operations on land.

H.M.S. *Jamaica* and *Black Swan* were despatched up the east coast to join a United States force in harassing the enemy's left flank. At dawn on 2nd July these ships were engaged in the first naval action of the war, when they were attacked by a force of six North Korean E-boats. The action was brief and decisive, all the E-boats being sunk except one.

On the same day, *Jamaica* joined in the first bombardment of the war. The ships continued harassing work, and it was during a bombardment that *Jamaica* suffered the first casualties of the war at sea when she was hit by a shell from a shore battery. It was most unfortunate that five of the six men killed were some soldiers from Hong Kong, who by their good conduct had been granted the privilege of joining this ship for the Navy's summer cruise. Meanwhile, on the west coast *Alacrity* started a patrol destined to grow into the west coast blockade which was, from the 5th July, the main task of the British Commonwealth ships and prevented supplies reaching the enemy by sea either from outside Korea or along the coast. *Triumph, Belfast* and the destroyers joined up with other American units and on 3rd July, only eight days after the British ships had been peacefully cruising off north Japan, the combined carrier force was in a position to fly off strikes over enemy territory.

From then onwards *Triumph* worked with the US 7th Fleet until the arrival of additional US carriers at the beginning of August enabled her to be released to join British Commonwealth forces blockading the west coast of Korea, where the aircraft were employed in seeking out and destroying enemy craft in the creeks and harbours.

By 5th July the British Commonwealth fleet had been reinforced by the British destroyers *Comus* and *Cockade*, the Australian destroyer *Bataan* and frigate *Shoalhaven*, with the Canadian destroyers *Cayuga, Athabaskan* and *Sioux* and the New Zealand frigates *Tutira* and *Pukaki* on passage to Japan. This contribution from the Commonwealth navies was considerable in relation to the size of their peacetime navies. The total number of officers and men of the navies of the British Commonwealth serving at this time in the Far East was about ten thousand, and of this number approximately seven thousand were engaged in operations in Korea: a very high percentage when the bases at Singapore and Hong Kong, and the naval commitments there, are taken into consideration.

There are always small difficulties to be overcome when the navies of two nations start working together, and it was most fortunate that the British ships had carried out joint manoeuvres with the US 7th Fleet earlier in the year. United States methods were adopted, and the Commander 7th Fleet chose to send a signal of congratulations to Rear-Admiral Andrewes on the 5th July on the excellent manner in which the British ships had taken to those methods.

Rear-Admiral Andrewes assumed responsibility for the west coast blockade on 5th July, and a United States Admiral was in command on the east coast. An escort force commanded by a Captain, Royal Navy, was also formed to convoy troopships and storeships to and from Japan, and both this and Admiral Andrewes's force was composed of ships belonging to the British Commonwealth. To carry out a blockade efficiently it must be 100 per cent and to achieve this means the continuous employment of a number of ships. At the commencement of the operation the ships available were few, so, therefore, they had to be kept on patrol to the maximum of their endurance; then a quick trip back to port, refuel and store and off again on patrol. The ships' crews had little time for shore leave, and the cheerful manner in which they carried out this arduous task was exemplary. The destroyers and frigates were often operating under difficult navigational conditions and in channels around the islands which had not been checked for many years.

The west coast of Korea is studded with small rocky islands and tortuous channels through which swirl fast and irregular tidal streams. For weeks on end the coast is shrouded in fog and during the winter months the bitterly cold winds blowing from Manchuria and Siberia cause rough weather in the Yellow Sea on five days out of seven. Most of the ports above the 38th parallel are icebound and, even when they were free, they could only be reached by navigating shallow channels easily mined by the enemy and often covered by shore batteries. Charts surveyed long ago were frequently out of date and a tidal range of more than thirty feet coupled with the silting of the larger river estuaries result in there being no guarantee that the ocean bed corresponded to the chart representation. From July 1951 the frigates H.M.S. *Cardigan Bay, Mounts Bay* and *Morecambe Bay* in the Han Estuary sounded twenty nine miles of channel in the estuary.

An officer wrote at this time: "A blockade patrol of ten to fourteen days on such a coast was never entirely dull and often provided excitement. The beat extended right up to the Yalu River. Apart from the ordinary patrolling to seek enemy craft, there were numerous opportunities for close inshore bombardment of enemy positions and lines of communications in support of our own forces.

"A typical day's work started with a destroyer on night patrol steaming to bombard a reported enemy troop position near the coast at first light. The hands were piped to action stations at 5.30 am and the guns prepared for the shoot as the ship crept through shoal waters in darkness. As soon as it was light enough for the spotter aircraft to observe the fall of shot, fire would be opened and continued until the target had been well covered or destroyed. The forenoon being spent directing minesweeping operations. Then it would be time to rendezvous with another ship and collect mail and despatches.

"These transfers of mail, and indeed anything from men to potatoes, are normally done at sea by jackstay, a line rigged between the two ships who steam parallel and close alongside each other while the particular commodity is hauled over on the jackstay. Such an operation requires a nice degree of seamanship, and in heavy weather determination.

"In the afternoon shore batteries would be engaged, with the fire directed by the ship's own spotting team landed in advance by boat. Another task would be to visit a friendly island and land stores and equipment for the garrison. At dusk ships would patrol the limits of prohibited night fishing areas, chasing the wayward friendly fisherfolk homewards in order to clear the seaward approaches and ease the detection of communist craft attempting to slip through the blockade. Nightfall finding the ships once again on patrol and sweeping the area with her radar.

"Later still there would be "contacts" - the "blips" detected on the ship's radar screen - which had to be investigated: the guns' crews would "stand to" while searchlights or starshells illuminated the area. The vessel thus disclosed might be identified as a friendly coaster supplying refugees on one of the off-lying islands. And if identity could not be so easily discovered, a whaler would be lowered to pull over with a boarding party for a thorough examination.

"Although east and west coasts were, broadly, American and British Commonwealth commitments, respectively, the two navies periodically exchanged one or more ships so that the destroyers and frigates also got their "run" on the east coast. Here the Communist main supply line and the end of the battle front ran along the coast and were easily accessible to ships. Operations were mainly in the Wonsan or Songjin area and a destroyer's time would be spent keeping up a running bombardment of road and rail communications both by day and night. A ship would usually fire over one thousand rounds from her main armament during a patrol and the consequent strain on her gun crews and equipment was considerable."

Inchon Landings

The British and Commonwealth ships played their full part. HM Cruisers *Jamaica, Ceylon* and *Triumph* providing air spotting, formed part of the bombarding force. The destroyers and frigates formed escorts and carried out close and outer screen duties at the port of Inchon. An eye-witness report from *Kenya* gives a visit idea of the accuracy of the bombarding ships. *Kenya* had been placed under the orders of an American Admiral and her bombardment was being spotted from an American plane.

"For our afternoon bombardment we had a spotter, a Corsair from the *Badoeng Strait,* and round about 1.30 he told us that we had scored two direct hits on the gun of our first target, so we shifted to some field guns. Within a couple of minutes we heard that we had destroyed a couple of them and also holed a tank which we had not known to be there. Some time later our spotter joyfully reported two more guns knocked out, but asked us to wait while he went down for a closer look. His report was: "One gun blown completely out of its emplacement, two on their sides, a fourth bent and chipped and a fire in an ammunition store." Less than ten minutes passed before our spotter found us another target. We opened up and after a few salvoes he reported:"Pretty, *Kenya.* Beautiful hit".

On completion of the Inchon landings Rear-Admiral Andrewes received the following signal from General MacArthur: "My heartiest congratulations on the splendid conduct of the Fleet Units under your command. They have added another glamourous page to the long and brilliant history of the Navies of the British Commonwealth."

Humanitarian Work

When the North Korean forces retreated north of the 38th parallel after the success of the Inchon landing and recapture of Seoul, many islands on the west coast had to be freed of isolated enemy garrisons. The local people were often desperately short of food. When H.M.S. *Ceylon* landed a party on Chaya-Ku-do near Inchon, they found a hut, in which were twenty orphaned children under the care of one woman. The temperature was below freezing. There was no fire, the children were almost naked and very sick. A message was sent back to the cruiser, and the Chaplain, the Reverend H. S. Fry, M.A., R.N., broadcast an appeal to the ship's company for gifts of surplus clothing. Within an hour his cabin was piled with offerings of shirts, coats and woollens. There were eager volunteers to man the next boat ashore, and it was noticed that men who went with it were bulging with parcels. Two "mercy" boats landed with food and clothing, a medical officer, Surgeon-Lieutenant H. E. G. Dyer, R.N., and the Chaplain.

Light Fleet Carriers

The Carriers *Triumph, Theseus, Glory* and *Ocean* served in turn in the west coast blockade. Squadrons of Sea Furies and Fireflies attacked enemy targets throughout the war. H.M.S. *Theseus*, for example, in December 1950 and January 1951 operated in close support of the British and United States troops on the west flank. A liaison officer was landed and stationed ashore with the 5th US Air Force. As many as 50 to 60 sorties were made a day in support of the ground forces. During a period of three weeks in December, 650 sorties were flown, and in a period of eight days in January 301 sorties were flown, and it was during the latter month that the 2,000th sortie during Korean operations was flown. During the above operations the total "bag" of destroyed targets included: 190 buildings occupied by enemy troops, 32 railway bridges, eight tunnels, 30 box cars, 21 trucks and lorries, five locomotives, 12 factories and warehouses, 5 power stations and 19 oil dumps.

The Battle of the Islands

The principal naval activity beyond the routine blockade duties was concerned with the security of certain islands fringing the west coast and in the river estuaries, some of strategic importance. Navigation among these islands was difficult owing to the ever-changing positions of shoals, insufficient navigational lights, and unreliability of charts.

The islands, garrisoned from time to time by irregular troops, frequently changed hands, the enemy possessing large numbers of small craft capable of traversing mined waters.

When UN land forces retreated in November 1950, the situation became critical. To galvanise the islands into some form of effective defensive measures and to co-ordinate Army and Air Force activities in the areas, the Commanding Officer of H.M.S. *Mounts Bay* organised a system of inshore and covering patrols towards the end of 1951. The task of the outer circle of ships was to keep the enemy approaches from Amgak and the Chinnampo estuary illuminated by starshell during critical periods in the dark hours, and this operation became known as "Smoking Concert" under the command of "Sitting Duck", otherwise the senior officer of the ships present - either H.M.S. *Mounts Bay* or H.M.S. *Whitesand Bay*. During November and early December the only island in the Yalu Gulf in the hands of friendly guerillas was Taewha-do, and an overseeing eye was kept on this and other friendly islands further south, notably Cho-do, Sok-to and Paengyang-do, which had been used as bases for raiding operations.

From December 1951, ships of the Commonwealth and United States Navies, assisted by small craft of the Republic of Korea Navy, fought a hundred days "Battle of the Islands" off the coast of Korea. The enemy began to invade the islands at the end of November. About 1,000 of them came in junks and small boats under covering fire from shore guns, and the lightly-held Taewha-do in the Yalu Gulf fell to them. H.M.S. *Cockade* sank several invading junks and one patrol vessel in this action and was herself under fire from the shore batteries. She suffered the loss of one Seaman killed.

Among the ships which have taken part in the operations were the British cruisers *Belfast* and *Ceylon, the USS Rochester* and *Manchester*; the British destroyers *Cossack, Cockade, Charity, Comus* and *Constance*; the Canadian destroyers *Cayuga, Athabaskan, Sioux* and *Nootka*; the Australian destroyers *Warramunga, Tobruk, Anzac* and *Bataan*, and the frigate *Murchison*; the Netherlands destroyer *Van Galen*; the British frigates *Mounts Bay, Whitesand Bay, Cardigan Bay* and *Alacrity*; the New Zealand frigates *Rotoiti, Taupo* and *Hawea*; and the US ships *Taussig, Fletcher, Porterfield, Eversole, Gurke* and *Comstock*; LST's and Rocket ships numbers *401, 403* and *404*, and tugs *Apache, Abnaki, Yuma* and *Arikari.*

Aircraft from the carrier *Glory*, the Australian light fleet carrier *Sydney*, and the US light carriers *Badoeng Strait* and *Bairoko* shared the duties of air support and reconnaissance. By day, under cover of the big guns of the cruisers, the destroyers and frigates went close inshore to shoot up suspected strong points and hunt out shore batteries. But the batteries were usually mobile and cleverly camouflaged and rarely did the enemy give themselves away to the watching aircraft. At night the ships took turns to illuminate the narrow channels between the islands and the mainland with starshells and rocket flares.

Seamen and Royal Marines from HM Ships along with US and Republic of Korea personnel patrolled in small boats investigating junks and keeping physical contact with the islands at night. Ship's radar swept the seas to locate enemy craft. Intense cold and a five-miles-wide track of pancake ice, some large enough to hole a ship, added to the difficulties of the operations. Temperatures fell to as low as nine degrees Fahrenheit. At times tugs had to be cut away through the ice for the warships to proceed.

By mid-March 1952 the Battle of the Islands had been won by U.N. Naval forces.

Rescue Work

The Navy frequently rescued downed American and British pilots. US Navy flyer Ensign Elmer McCallum swam to a rock nearby and tried to hide from the enemy looking for him. He was shouted to all night. Next morning a large motor-boat came out and McCallum thought that this time he would be taken prisoner. However, the British forces had been told of his 'ditching', and H.M.S. *Cockade* was sent to his rescue. At about the time that the motor-boat was getting ready to land her crew on the island, H.M.S. *Cockade* appeared over the horizon at top speed towards the rock on which McCallum was hiding. A shot landed in the water near the motor-boat, and deciding that further investigation would be foolish, it turned towards the shore and made off. He was soon safe aboard *Cockade.*

On another occasion in April 1951, H.M.S. *Cockade* and a friendly Korean junk co-operated in rescue. Nearing the junk among the shallows it was seen that the crew were waving white flags and gesticulating, they then held up a black cloth inscribed in white: "Have American on board". Once alongside the junk the destroyer was able to haul on board a very unkempt and bearded figure in tattered uniform bearing the mud-covered flash of the U.S.A.F., who reported himself as Lieutenant Donald S. Thomas, senior, and added, "Boy, I am glad to see you". As this officer unfolded his story it was clear that the nondescript occupants of the junk were responsible for having saved his life, at no small danger to themselves. The word went around the ship's company and showers of chocolates, cigarettes and other comforts were thrown into the junk.

A most unusual rescue task took place in July 1951 - the recovery of a crashed Russian built MIG-15 aircraft, the presence of which had been reported in shallow waters south-west of Hanchon. This was some 100 miles behind the enemy lines. The wreckage was sighted and, not without difficulty, the position fixed by Sea Furies of No. 804 Squadron from H.M.S. *Glory* on 11th and 13th July. The position of the crashed aircraft was well within range of enemy air bases. The surrounding area consisted of shoals and mudbanks which, with the treacherous tide, made navigation hazardous. The approach to the crashed aircraft lay up a forty mile narrow channel bounded by sandbars. It was evident that the recovery must be made by small craft, covered from the nearest deep water channel by a frigate. H.M.S. *Cardigan Bay* was allotted this task and cover from seaward was supplied by aircraft from H.M.S. *Glory* and H.M.S. *Kenya*. For the actual recovery a shallow draught landing craft (L.S.U.) was made available by the U.S. Navy.

At first light on 20th July H.M.S. *Cardigan Bay*, leading a South Korean motor-boat and the L.S.U., set off up the channel. Navigation was assisted by Sea Furies from H.M.S. *Glory* who flew along the channel to indicate deep water. At the end of the main channel H.M.S. *Cardigan Bay* lowered her motor-boat with Lieutenant M. Ross, RN, in charge. This boat led the South Korean motor-boat and the L.S.U., piloted by Sub-Lieutenant R. M. Nicholls, RN, to the wrecked aircraft. Operations could only be conducted at low water which was about 1700. However, the team from H.M.S. *Cardigan Bay* together with the U.S. naval crew of the L.S.U. and army and airforce technicians who had been specially embarked, worked with such a will that nearly all parts found had been collected when darkness set in. At 0400 on 21st July work started again and, the morning tide being lower, more parts were found and recovered.

The enemy made no attempt to interfere with the operation, although aircraft from U.S.S. *Sicily*, who had taken over from H.M.S. *Glory*, drew light heavy AA fire when they dived on batteries only a mile from the scene. On completion of the operation and for good measure, the guns of H.M.S. *Cardigan Bay* and aircraft from U.S.S. *Sicily* combined to score directed hits on an enemy gun position. The whole party withdrew successfully to Chado on 21st July.

The UN Command attached great importance to the recovery of this aircraft and it was generally referred to as 'the million dollar baby'. The British participants however, preferred the title 'The Crown Jewels' a reference to a similar, but less successful salvage operation undertaken in other coastal waters by King John.

Fleet Air Arm Versus MIG-15s

In July 1952, MIG-15s, based in Manchuria and so safe from attack until they left the frontier of Communist China, attacked British naval aircraft for the first time. Four Fireflies of H.M.S. *Ocean* were attacked by two MIGs, two of the Fireflies being damaged. One landed safely on board, and the other on a friendly airstrip. The crews were uninjured. Shortly afterwards four Sea Furies were attacked by four MIGs. The encounter was brief, and no Sea Furies were damaged.

In August, H.M.S. *Ocean's* Sea Furies had four more encounters with MIG-15s. On 9th August, four Sea Furies were attacked by eight MIGs at 5,000 feet. After a brief but spirited action one MIG was destroyed, exploding as it hit the ground, and repeated hits with 20mm cannon were obtained on two others which then broke off the action and, screened by the remaining five, retired to the northward. No damage was sustained by the Sea Furies. On the same day, four Sea Furies were attacked by four MIGs at 6,000 feet. One MIG broke away emitting black smoke and flames, and the remaining three broke off the action. One Sea Fury was hit during this engagement, one of his drop tanks being set on fire. Later he managed to jettison his blazing tank, put out the fire by side slipping and made a safe deck landing. An hour later a third action occurred between two Sea Furies and two MIGs at 4,000 feet. One Sea Fury was hit and had to make a forced landing on a friendly island. The pilot was uninjured. The next day, four Sea Furies were attacked by eight MIGs. One MIG broke away smoking and on fire, but could not be claimed as a 'certain' as no-one saw it crash. No Sea Furies were damaged.

Chapter 6

THE ROYAL MARINES

By the Editors

A special Royal Marine Independent Commando was sent out to Japan early in the war. The Royal Marine Commandos are picked men from the Corps, and carry out a period of special training. When not attached to the Commandos, they serve in ships of the Royal Navy. These troops are specially trained for raids on enemy communications behind the front line. Suitable targets were few, but they carried out a number of raids, operating from ships of the United Nations. When the Inchon invasion took place they carried out a diversionary landing at Junsan from the British frigate *Whitesand Bay* alongside American special troops.

The toughest fight of 41 Independent Commando took place in November and December 1950 when, under the command of Lieutenant-Colonel J. B. Drysdale, it was sent to assist the US 1 Marine Division in occupying the north east of Korea, north of the port of Hungnam. When the Division's road link with Hungnam was cut by encircling Chinese forces, Lieutenant-Colonel Drysdale was put in command of a combined American and British task force. From Hungnam, they fought their way through the mountain passes, and at one time had Chinese Communists firing into the vehicles from the ditches six yards away at the side of the road. It was here that the Commando was split, their rear party being cut off when a phosphorus bomb set fire to the ammunition truck. This made it impossible for the following vehicles to continue up the road. A part of this story was told by one of the wounded, Marine James A. Stanley, of West Bromwich, Staffordshire: "The early North American covered wagon stories had nothing on this convoy", Stanley said. "Nothing as bad as this ever happened to me before", and he added that Lieutenant-Colonel Drysdale had told him the convoy was the worst experience he had had in his career. Colonel Drysdale served with the Commandos during World War Two. Marine Stanley was then serving with small operations groups and was engaged in operations from submarines at Arakan, Burma, Nicobar Islands, Sumatra, Malaya and Singapore.

Stanley went on to say: "A few hours after we started from Hungnam for Hagaru, Lieutenant-Colonel Drysdale's jeep was fired on by Communists but no one was injured. The jeep was well ahead of the main body at the time. We were told that there was an ambush ahead and we were put into camp. We dug in until daybreak, expecting an attack. Then we were told to clear the hills of guerillas. We changed our socks for spare socks which we kept inside our clothing, and we shook out the ice from our boots before putting them on again. I've been in Iceland, Norway and Russia, but I have never known cold like that night. Then we took the first hill, losing two men wounded by sniping. The US Marines went through us to the second hill. Soon afterwards tanks of the American 7th US Marines came up and it was decided to push the convoy through up the road behind them. The convoy was composed of reinforcements for the 7th US Marines, some US Army and ourselves. We were 230 strong, being driven in American trucks, having left our drivers behind to pick up our transport when it arrived.

"We started off about noon, and it was pretty quiet for the first two miles. Then the Communists gave us all they had got. They were using burp guns and machine-guns. They were in the ditches alongside the road, sometimes only six yards away. The jeep in front of us had three drivers killed in one hour. They hit the ammunition truck with a phosphorus bomb and set it on fire. This cut off the rest of the Commando trucks which were behind it. I was in the one just ahead of the ammunition truck, and we kept going until we joined the 7th US Marines at Hagaru at 11 pm. We were mustered and there were 63 of us present. That night 55 more Commandos fought their way through and reached us. The Communists were in the hills all around the camp at Hagaru. We rested a while and prepared to attack in the morning. Only sniping took place the next day, but at 11 pm the US Marines on the left flank, on a hill near the camp entrance, were pushed back. The 32 of us in 'B' Company were sent up to retake the left flank of the hill, and we did it just before dawn. I saw dozens of dead Communists from where we were; they must have been thousands round the defence perimeter." Two mornings later Stanley was wounded in the arm by a sniper.

Finally, Drysdale's force became the rearguard for the retreat of the US Marines through enemy held country. The break out to Hungnam and evacuation by sea took six days during which Drysdale's men suffered much from harassing fire, lack of food and sleep and exposure to bitter cold winds. 41 Commando lost 13 men killed, 39 wounded and 27 missing. They were eventually awarded a Presidential Unit Citation.

Lieutenant-Colonel Drysdale and his men returned to North Korea in April 1951. A raiding force of 250 Royal Marine Commandos stormed ashore at 8 am on April 7 eight miles south of Songjin and demolished a section of the mainline of the coastal railway. The Commandos, operating as part of a Combined Task Force under the overall command of Rear-Admiral Roscoe H. Hillenkoetter, USN, succeeded in blowing up more than 100 yards of railway track and left a crater 16 feet deep.

The mission was accomplished under cover of naval aircraft and a bombardment force including the US heavy cruiser, *Saint Paul.* A fire control party from the *Saint Paul* accompanied the Royal Marines ashore and throughout the operations directed supporting naval gun fire while the Commandos maintained a defence perimeter and planted their demolition charges.

Although a captured civilian reported strong anti-invasion forces to the north at Songjin,the raiding party encountered only token resistance and small arms fire during the seven hours required to complete the task. So complete was the surprise of the landing and so effective was the curtain of naval gunfire in denying the enemy access to the area that no casualties were suffered.

Chapter 7

THE WOMEN'S VOLUNTARY SERVICE

By Ashley Cunningham-Boothe

History shows that the first recorded conception of what was needed to combat the sheer boredom of wartime soldiering overseas was for men to "see and talk to English women, who must be good-looking, gay and compassionate people but who, nevertheless, knew how to behave and would not get too friendly with the men", and is credited to a Welfare Officer (later to become an ordained minister of the church) serving with the Eighth Army in North Africa, who proposed this at a meeting of General Montgomery's Chiefs of staff, at which he was responsible for taking notes of the proceedings.

"Where does one find such rare birds?" was the first disapproving response that ridiculed the Welfare Officer's suggestion. Then, someone else said, "Lady Reading has started a movement called the WVS which seems to be flexible and ready to try out what seems to be required at the moment. Why don't we ask her?"

WVS (Services Welfare) members were civilians, who were sponsored for the most part by NAAFI. It might well be said of this that it was one of their main sources of strength, since they were able to cut across the barriers which differences of rank inevitably create within the Armed Services.

When the War Office, being mindful of Article 43 in the 1949 Geneva Convention, asked the WVS for a table of rank/title/appointment, indicating where possible their status in relation to ranks in the army (helpfully attaching a copy of their own hierarchy from Field Marshal downwards) the W.V.S. sent back a list of only four appointments in their organization: WVS Administrator (senior WVS member serving in each command) then Area Organizer followed by Club Organizer and, lastly, Welfare Worker, who may work alone or in teams. Thus illustrating their simplicity of purpose and of command and administration, which seemed to encourage them not to look for complications to the problems of themselves living in wartime conditions abroad or of the problems imaginary or real of the soldier-clients

WVS in Korea

The first two British women to serve in Korea following the outbreak of war were members of the WVS and were sent there in November 1951, joining the 1st Commonwealth Division base camp at Pusan, where they lived in conditions that can only be described as harsh and primitive.

The first 'club' to be established by these women was in a room in a hut, which history now records of the experience: "in the most glorious muddle of masculine disorder."

Later, they were to be joined by other WVS ladies, but never more than eight of them were to serve in Korea during their continued commitment to the welfare of British and Commonwealth troops from 1951 until 1957, during which time they extended their activities to Inchon (once the scene of General MacArthur's audacious assault landing by United Nations Forces in 1950) where a 'club' was established at the Commonwealth Division Rest Centre, catering for the needs of men who were to spend three days rest and relaxation (R and R leave) in the one-time 'Lido' that had been used by Japanese naval officers during their occupation of Korea. From here they operated their 'Rover Service' to troops in the forward area, near the 38th Parallel; riding quite long distances in open jeeps, an experience which even seasoned campaigners found daunting; through snowstorms and bitterly-cold, sub-zero winter conditions or through clouds of thick dust thrown up by vehicles ahead of them on the MSR (main supply route), during the 'dry' season, as they went about distributing their wares for the troops and taking and executing for them 'say it with flowers' messages to loved ones at home. They also worked in Seoul, the capital city of South Korea, where they organized excursions to places of interest for those on R and R leave. Running the recreation room at Inchon, where 16,000 troops passed through each month, were Miss Hilda Hickley Wood of Derby and Miss Patricia Whittal of London. Until 1953, they were probably the only British women in uniform in Korea. As well as organizing games and competitions and other activities, they helped to package gift-parcels being sent home by troops.

Service personnel entrained to the forward area and passing through Seoul received visits from these ladies, handing out magazines and a variety of creature comforts.

WVS involvement in the repatriation of ex-prisoners-of-war returning to the United Kingdom from Korea.

Operation 'Homeward Bound' gave those serving with the WVS in Korea "a wonderful opportunity in welfare work" during the time of intense excitement and in the turmoil of emotion for repatriated British POWs experiencing their first day of freedom, reassuring them that they had not been forgotten by either their loved ones or the British people.

Men gripped the hands of the WVS ladies so tightly that it hurt, often without so much as a single word being uttered between them; the men overwhelmed by the aroused emotion of the occasion and of simply being able to touch an Englishwoman. "The look in their eyes a joy to see".

The total number of British POWs who passed through Britannia Camp was 1,005, arriving there at the rate from two to ninety, on twenty six days out of the thirty two day period of prisoner release.

One highlight of recollection of those times was when the two WVS, acting as barmaids, put down a glass of frothy, ice-cold beer (courtesy of the NAAFI) in front of each returning POW, and the light in their eyes will always be remembered by the WVS ladies involved.

The popularity of the 'say it with flowers' service kept the two women busy sending them to mothers and wives and girl friends. Writing letters, too, for the returning POWs often kept the two women busy writing by the light of candles or electric torch for hours on end. Over one hundred letters were written to their womenfolk by the ladies of the WVS in Korea.

Hilda Hickley Wood spent thirteen months in Korea - the longest spell served by any member of her organization. She returned to the UK aboard the troopship *Empire Pride* and arrived in Liverpool in March 1953. Her service in Korea had commenced in January 1952, and she was one of six WVS personnel dealing with the welfare of 17,000 British and Commonwealth troops, often working twelve hours a day and with no days off. Her work also took her on visits to the United Nations Cemetery at Pusan, following requests from bereaved for the WVS to place flowers on the graves of loved ones.

Miss Hilda Wood, WVS, at Pusan in 1952. In 1953, she married Captain P. A. Downward, DFC. She died in 1976.

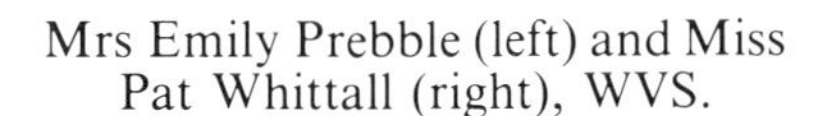

Mrs Emily Prebble (left) and Miss Pat Whittall (right), WVS.

C. Bogart

1st Bn. Argyll and Sutherland Highlanders on *HMS Ceylon* arriving at Pusan, 29th August 1950.

Charles Bogart of the Argyll's. A self-portrait in the campaign. Today, he is the piper for BKVA.

C. Bogart

The crossing over the frozen Han river east of Seoul which most of 27 Brigade used to withdraw south on 3-4 January 1951. Probably a view from the north bank.

C. Bogart
Refugees walking south from Uijongbu as the Chinese army advanced, 1st January 1951.

R. Stevens

A trapped Russian built T34 tank near Suwon

R. Stevens

The L.A.D. unit of the R.E.M.E. at work.

R. Stevens

L.A.D. lorry in trouble. The white circle denotes 29 Brigade.

R. Stevens

Cholera inoculations, March 1951

R. Stevens

"Margie", a lost Korean girl, was also inoculated.

R. Stevens

"Margie", dressed in clothes sent from England by Sgt. R. Stevens' wife, ready to be taken to an orphanage in October 1951.

Brigadier T. Brodie with the Royal Ulster Rifles

Ulster Crossing over the Imjin river.

A. T. Eeles

Pintail bridge over the Imjin, September 1951. In 1952, a high level steel bridge was built by US Corps of Engineers.

Lieut.-Colonel K. O. N. Foster, D.S.O., O.B.E., who commanded 1st Bn. Royal Northumberland Fusiliers, was killed during the Battle of the Imjin.

Royal Northumberland Fusiliers, November 1950. Fusilier Fred Smith is marked.

Ashley Cunningham-Boothe, RNF, after the Battle of the Imjin. The desk was taken from Seoul University and the space heater (right) supplied by the Americans.

Lord Westmeath

A 25 pounder of 45 Field Regiment, Royal Artillery.

R. Barnett

Gunner Simpson, 70 Battery, holding the 100,000 round to be fired by 45 Field Regiment on 8 September 1951.

M. White

A 4.2 inch mortar of 42 Battery, 61 Light Regiment, R.A.

A. Carter

A 4.2 inch mortar of 120 Battery

P. J. Brindley
"Hoochies" of B. Squadron, 5 Royal Inniskilling Dragoon Guards, December 1951. Note sleeping bags hanging on line.

P. J. Brindley
A Centurion tank of B. Squadron 5 R.I.D.G. with a track off in Gloucester Valley.

I. T. Stratford
A Centurion tank of A Squadron 5 R.I.D.G. hull down on 159, November 1952.

Cromwell tanks were used for reconnaissance in the earlier part of the war.

Ian Stratford, R. Signals attached 5 R.I.D.G. visits Peter Farrar, 1 Bn. R. Fusiliers, 18 November 1952.

I. T. Stratford

The "basha" slept in by Signalman Stratford. Beer crates serve as "window" frames. November 1952.

I. T. Stratford

Inside the "basha". Note Sten gun, rubber soled boot, primitive bed and stove made from an oil drum and burning diesel oil.

I. T. Stratford

355 seen from the rear of 159 in a snow covered landscape, 3 December 1952

I. T. Stratford

View north from 355 towards Chinese held 317, scene of fierce fighting in 1951.

I. T. Stratford

The barrel of the Centurion points along the "mad mile" toward Chinese held 227 (John), on the left beyond the grim hulk of 355.

P. J. Brindley
A typical thatched house in a village behind the line. A few simple things are laid out for sale. Trooper Howe, 5 R.I.D.G.

E. E. Holloway
64 Field Park Squadron, Royal Engineers. L/Cpl. Burdett.

E. E. Holloway

The electricity generating unit of a workshop troop, Royal Engineers. Known as "Bertram Mills' Circus".

A Scammel of 10 Infantry Workshops R.E.M.E. which drove over an enemy mine in 1951.

J. Weldrick
10 Infantry Workshops, south of the Imjin, 1952.

N. Pope
R.E.M.E. at work.

H. Buckley
Field bakery, 1951. Note Sten gun against the wall.

P. Farrar
Mortar platoon, 1 Bn. R. Fusiliers, washing string vests and "long johns" with the aid of immersion heaters, January 1953.

P. Farrar
Mortar platoon, R. Fusiliers, "hoochie" in 28 Brigade Reserve Area, January 1953. Note newly made "thunder box" to be placed over a pit dug on the top of a hill.

T. Phillips
Urinals made from the outer casings of 20 pound Centurion shells were standard throughout the Commonwealth Division.

N. Pope

N.A.A.F.I. Mobile Canteen visiting 45 Field Regiment, R.A., 1951.

P. Farrar

The static line allowed the N.A.A.F.I. to build several roadhouses like Newmarket Roadhouse on the main supply route to Seoul.

D. J. Hill, R.F.
A wounded Royal Fusilier is laid in the stretcher pannier of a U.S. Army helicopter at a strip by 159.

L. U. Pedersen
The Norwegian Mobile Advanced Surgical Hospital which served I US Army Corps including the Commonwealth Division.

P. Farrar

A Communist Chinese made 7.62 mm calibre "burp gun" of Russian design, captured by the R. Fusiliers. It weighs 12 pounds.

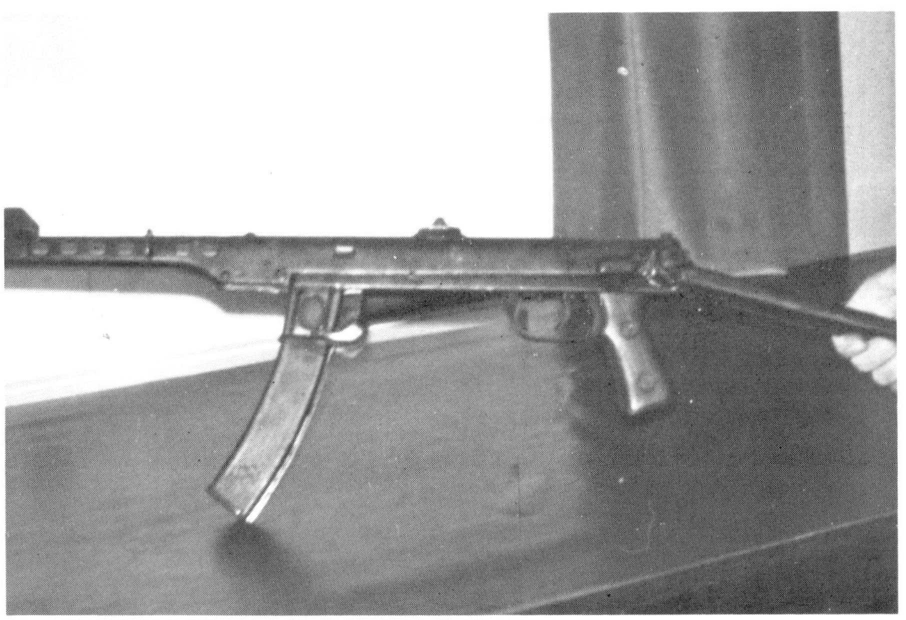

P. Farrar

Another common weapon used by the Communist Chinese was this 7.62 mm calibre sub-machine gun. It weighs 8 pounds loaded.

Brigadier George Taylor D.S.O., 28 Commonwealth Brigade, September 1951. He was not wearing his medal ribbons.

PART II

PERSONAL EXPERIENCES

Chapter 8

DRUMMER EAGLES: FRAGMENTS OF HISTORY

By Ashley Cunningham-Boothe

Drummer Eagles goes to war

During the great "bug out" of UN forces from North Korea after the massive Chinese intervention of November 1950, Drummer Tony Eagles had the first of several testing experiences, which became entrenched in his mind for ever.

With others from his unit - The Gloucestershire Regiment - they had been ordered to keep open two bridges that were vital for the withdrawal of UN forces; following which they were to be destroyed, so as to slow down the Red push. Leaving the city of Pyongyang the 3-ton Bedford truck carrying Tony Eagles and others were halted by the Adjutant of the Regiment, Captain Anthony Farrar-Hockley. He ordered Drum Major Buss to detail two men to take charge of another 3-tonner loaded with four unserviceable motor-cycles, telling him that they were to be delivered to the Battalion's new positions - "just down the road!"

Drummer Eagles and Private Jones were detailed. Then came the good news: the 3-tonner, as well as the motor-cycles, was unserviceable due to a broken camshaft. However, the Drum Major's words that all bode well, because 'A' Company, who were bringing up the rear, had a tank-transporter in their column, providing the tow, offered some reassurance to the two men. It came as a surprise, therefore, when 'A' Company arrived with the tank-transporter already carrying one vehicle and towing another! When the frustrated two-some enquired of the crew of the tank-transporter how they should get their crippled 3-tonner to the Battalion's new positions - and God knows where they were! - they were not endeared by the derisive comment: "We don't give a damn! Don't you know there's a bloody war going on?" shouted at them as the TRV disappeared down the Main Supply Route, leaving Drummer Eagles and Private Jones to contemplate the misery of their situation by the disappearing last-light of the day. And darkness in wartime can have the most alarming effect upon men, even those who, otherwise, are seen to be resolute.

Sympathetic Americans, driving hell-for-leather down the MSR, did little to reassure them as they bawled: "Get your ass out of there - the Commies are coming!" Eventually, though, a 2½-ton GMC truck - popularly known as a 'Deuce-and-a-half,' driven by a black American, stopped and offered them a lift. Instead of abandoning the 3-tonner, however, they pleaded with the driver to tow it; telling him that they would surely be court-martialled and suffer imprisonment if they failed to obey their Adjutant's orders; stressing how very different things were in the British Army. So, convinced, the American then agreed to tow them. This was the moment of truth for Tony Eagles and his chum - for they discovered that neither one of them could drive!

Necessity being the mother of invention, Tony grabbed the driver's wheel. So commenced a nightmare journey through the darkness, with only the tail-lights of the 'Deuce-and-a-half' to guide him and to keep him from steering his vehicle down any one of the many deep-sided ravines as they traversed steep escarpments along the MSR.

The American belonged to a transport company called "The Wolfhounds". When they stopped at a village for food and to refuel the vehicles, Private Jones discovered that both their rifles had been stolen by souvenir-hunting American soldiers. This added to their miserable experiences - for the British soldier is indoctrinated from 'day one' of his service into believing that he is naked without his personal firearm, and losing it was an invitation to a court-martial. The rifles were never recovered.

After assisting with the refuelling of vehicles in the convoy, Tony Eagles returned to the crippled truck and discovered that, in his absence, the Drum Major had turned up in a truck, hooked-up the 3-tonner and, with Private Jones also in tow, had gone off to the Battalion, leaving a message with the Americans: "Drummer Eagles should make his own way back to the Regiment!"

Due to a misunderstanding and a confused situation, "The Wolfhounds" moved off without the young Drummer; and the Chinese,quite literally, "just down the road!" Henceforth, only Korean refugees passed through the village. One Korean elder wearing a Kat (a traditional black horse-hair hat) confirmed his worst fears that the Reds were just shouting-distance along the road. He thanked the elder, then made off in great haste along the MSR.

He heard the deep rumbling roar of an explosion and, when he reached the river, was horrified to come across a bridge that had just been demolished by Engineers, seen speeding away in a jeep, but too far off to pay heed to his cries for help.

Studying the twisted wreckage, he realized that it would be possible, if somewhat difficult, to negotiate a crossing. On reaching the other side, he was immediately approached by an old Korean woman, who indicated in sign language that there was a woman in labour nearby. One glance at the pregnant woman showed the foetal-skull prominently exposed. He realized that delivery was imminently threatening. First, he reassured the woman with calming-strokes to her brow, until the girl-child thrust its way into the war. He cut the umbilical cord and washed the baby in the nearby river.

Handing the baby back to the mother, he covered them both with an American greatcoat he had taken from a supply dump at Pyongyang, bade them farewell, and resumed his journey south at a brisk pace.

At the end of the day he had reached a small town paunched by the swollen tide of humanity escaping from the terror of war. Here he was approached by a group of young Korean Christians, who asked him to join them. He took them to be students, for they spoke good English.

Having eaten and then taken his first sleep for days, he was awakened by the rude shakings of his companions and greeted with the news that the Chinese were almost upon them. In haste, but with controlled equanimity, he and the others departed the town by way of its narrow lanes until they reached a river. In the grey light of early morning he could see that there was no bridge in either direction. He prepared himself mentally for the swim, but one of the young women took his hand and told him to place his feet exactly where she would place her's as they crossed the river on unseen stepping-stones just a few inches below the surface, yet not visible to the eye.

Part way across the river, he could not help wondering what they looked like from a distance - Christ-like - walking the waters!

They had travelled barely a mile beyond the river when the sound of horses warned them of approaching enemy soldiers. This was accompanied by loud voices and the strident sounds blasted out of bugles and by the rat-a-tat noise of automatic gunfire. The girl travelling with Tony Eagles explained that this was the usual pattern of events when Chinese soldiers entered a town or village; killing everyone and anything that moved; raping females of all ages. She told him that her sister had taken her own life after she and some friends had been repeatedly raped by North Korean soldiers. The quality of her hatred for the enemy soldiers altered an otherwise gentle face into one contorted by her loathing.

The Listening Patrol

29 Brigade occupied positions south of the River Imjin; the 'Glosters' were entrenched on hills to the west of a narrow valley, which gave direct access to Seoul, the capital city of South Korea. The way the enemy would come.

HQ Company of this famous British Regiment were dug-in on Hill 235. And it was from this Company that Drummer Anthony Eagles and Private Hunter, under the leadership of Corporal George Cook, were selected to carry out a Listening Patrol on the south bank of the Imjin.

The formality was straightforward and uncomplicated: by jeep to Hill 148, occupied by 'A' Company, then on foot to the river. Corporal Cook was to set up a listening post in a vantage point that would screen them from enemy eyes, yet permit an unobstructed view of the ford; this was were the enemy would be expected to cross, set up a field telephone link with TAC HQ, then spend the night watching and straining the ears for the familiar sounds of troop movement.

Earlier, a Reconnaissance Patrol had crossed the river and advanced about 35 miles north, but at the end of the day reported little enemy activity. Certainly, Corporal Cook and the others were not expecting to occupy ringside seats or become involved in the action against the enemy precursory to one of the major battles fought in that war; one that was to be recorded in the annals of their Regiment and in the annals of British military history - the Battle of the River Imjin.

The Gloucestershire Regiment, supported by 'C' Troop, 170 Mortar Battery, RA, would eventually receive the American Presidential Unit Citation for their outstanding conduct and courage in that battle. Sitting in his foxhole on the banks of the Imjin, Tony Eagles certainly never expected to read an account of this epic battle in the Shanghai News in a prisoner of war camp in North Korea!

Though the worst of winter was past, the April nights were still bone-chilling and bitterly cold, but the clear night provided excellent visibility. And the young Drummer passed the hours away thinking of home and wondering whether or not Stanley Matthews would win a coverted 'Winner's Medal' and, in a few days hence, what it would be like in Tokyo, Japan, where he was to spend 5 days R and R (rest and recuperation) leave. His mind was a scurrying activity of thoughts and imagination.

2200 hours: Drummer Eagles nudged Private Hunter, his attention attracted by the movement of troops farther along the opposite bank, searching for the ford. However, the only known crossing-point was in line with where the Listening Patrol had positioned itself. Corporal Cook reported a 14-man patrol to his Adjutant, Captain Anthony Farrar-Hockley, who then made contact with the Gunners and asked them to illuminate the sky with flares above the river. He wanted to be sure that the movement reported by the Listening Patrol was, without doubt, just an enemy patrol.

The bright artificial light of the flares exposed the enemy soldiers, and Corporal Cook confirmed this. The three men remained quiet and continued to report the enemy movement: the golden rule for a listening patrol. Captain Farrar-Hockley, however, had other ideas. He ordered Corporal Cook to engage the enemy and to prevent them from gaining a foothold on the south bank.

The Private and the Drummer debated between themselves how best they should deal with the enemy: they mutually agreed to wait until the enemy reached close quarters and a point of "can't miss 'em", when they would lob grenades amongst them, steal the advantage and create maximum casualties before firing their rifles. After all, it was concluded, the odds were almost 5 to 1 in favour of the enemy. Within hours, though, such odds would seem infinitestimal compared with the vast numbers of Chinese troops that would engage 29 Brigade and their Regiment. They reassured each other that, though they were only three in number, their training made them vastly superior to their adversaries; in fact, made them better soldiers!

The Adjutant advised Corporal Cook to engage the enemy as soon as they reached half-way point crossing the river; so targets were marked as they waited for the order to open fire; permitting the Adjutant the advantage of his strategy. George Cook's quiet mannerism and his matter-of-fact confidence had a steadying influence on the other two; the kind that gives that all-important and pyschological 'helping-hand' to those inexperienced in battle; that which is an integral part of the great purpose of leadership - regardless of rank.

Taking his cue from the Adjutant, Corporal Cook gave the order to open fire. Drummer Eagles saw his first target topple over; the lifeless or badly-injured body carried away by the swift-flowing waters of the river; and for one brief moment his thoughts were for the enemy, and what it must be like on the receiving-end of all those bullets.

Over the telephone link, Captain Farrar-Hockley demanded to know why they had taken a Bren-gun with them on a Listening Patrol. Corporal Cook reassured the Adjutant that it was no Bren-gun - it was Hunter and Eagles firing their rifles at a furious rate!

Other soldiers were seen to fall below the surface of the water, as the three 'Glosters' poured rifle-fire into the ill-fated enemy patrol; some disappearing altogether; others screaming the tormented cries of the wounded, as bullets tore into their bodies. Walking-wounded were aided by their comrades to the far bank. The order was given to cease fire.

Reloaded, the three spent the remainder of that night in a state of nervous apprehension, expecting the enemy to return in force and attack them. They were relieved, therefore, when the enemy had not done so by first light, and they were ordered to return to the comparative safety of Battalion HQ, and make their report.

At much the same time, an Ambush Patrol had been sent across the Imjin to make contact with the enemy and bag a prisoner for interrogation. They were attacked by a superior force and exhausted their ammunition as they made good their escape. It was April 22nd 1951. During the night of 22nd/23rd April the Chinese crack 63rd Army launched the attack on 29 Brigade. By noon on the 25th the 'Glosters', spent of ammunition and completely surrounded by numerically superior forces, were obliged by these circumstances to lay down their arms. For them, the battle and the war was over. The Chinese may have bagged the 'Glorious Glosters', but more important, history too had bagged its entry for the annals.

Escape and Recapture

During the Chinese Army's spring offensive - 21st to 25th April 1951 - men of the Royal Northumberland Fusiliers, the Royal Ulster Rifles, the Royal Artillery and other supporting units making up 29 Brigade, as well as those who, like Drummer Anthony Eagles, served with the Gloucestershire Regiment, were captured during the battle of the Imjin River. And to reach the POW camps, which were situated near the Yalu River, where North Korea borders with China (Manchuria); and to avoid being straffed or bombed by UN aircraft, the captives were forcemarched some 30 miles each night along the dusty, unsurfaced road that meandered through the seclusion of the Korean wilderness and through miles of mountainous terrain.

Gathered up along the way were several American soldiers. Of these, two joined a group of Drummers from the 'Glosters,' accompanied by the huge figure of Ron Allum of 'B' company. During the conversation that took place, two Americans - one nicknamed 'Blackie' and the other 'Davey,' but their proper names were Blackwell and Davies - proposed a plan of escape and invited Tony Eagles and Ron Allum to join them. Their plan was to make for the coast where, hopefully, they would be able to commandeer a craft of sorts and put to sea. It was argued that they would stand a far better chance at sea, and of being spotted by one of the many UN naval ships operating in Korean waters off the west coast.

Both Americans had previously attempted to escape, but had been recaptured, and were desperate to make another attempt. The only detail that Tony Eagles is able to recollect about the Americans is that they were captured during November 1950 and had, rather astonishingly so, survived the most appalling winter conditions, despite being always on the move. This was a great credit to their versatility and their tenacity and their desire for survival.

They told of the hundreds of their comrades who had perished in captivity due to the causes of dysentry and malnutrition and by the general deprivation of creature comforts as well as from the severe cold, but this added to their grim determination to attempt another escape, or to die in their approval of the attempt.

The plan of escape required them to slip away from the column, in silent evanescence, whenever the opportunity presented itself, each following the other, and to hide in the undergrowth until the column had passed. They would then signal each other with imitated owl hoots; reminding themselves of the need to ensure that all "tail-end-Charlies" - always in evidence by the very nature of their injuries and illness - had finally gone by, before giving out with the recognition call. It was further agreed that they should each deny any charge of collusion in the escape plot, in the event that they were re-captured, for they were sure to be punished if the enemy thought this; so they agreed the story that one had fallen by the wayside with illness (proving to be strangely prophetic, as things transpired) and one other had stopped to offer assistance; then these two were eventually discovered by the other two, who would claim to have been "tail-end-Charlies"; all would agree to have lost their bearings in the dark wilderness in their attempt to rejoin the column.

That night they travelled along a narrow footway that threaded its way through the foothills. Eventually, they came to ground more densely covered with scrub than usual. Tony Eagles took the initiative and slipped away into the shadows and the nearby scrub. By whispering word of mouth, Ron Allum learned that the Eagle had flown. So, too, did Blackwell and Davies; each following the other into the low underwood.

Satisfied that all the "tail-end-Charlies" had gone by, Drummer Eagles gave out with the sound of an owl hoot, muted, so that it would not travel far on the night air. In unison the others answered the call. As he quietly called their names, their shadowy forms emerged from the penurious thicket, each from a different direction, and moments later, they were on their way.

Diffused starlight made conditions ideal for night travel as they moved on in a westerly direction until dawn, when they came across a wooded area on fairly high ground, affording them shelter and protection from unfriendly eyes. For two more days and nights they did much the same sort of thing: always heading in a westerly direction and never travelling in daylight, so as to avoid detection.

On the morning of the fourth day, as they rested, the day became sunny and hot. Three took refuge from the scorching rays of the sun, but Ron Allum soaked it up and fell asleep. By mid-afternoon he became quiet ill, presumably from sunstroke. Prior to their escape, it was agreed that, if one of them became incapacitated by illness or injury, the others would leave him behind. Yet, when misfortune struck, they found it impossible to abandon their comrade.

Discussing this new development, they agreed that the first priority was to find a source of water for Ron, so that he would not suffer from dehydration. Then they would decide what next to do. They moved off immediately, although it was daylight, thus breaking the rule for survival - never to move during daytime. But the condition of their fellow escapee concerned them greatly, and they felt the risk was justifiable.

Traversing the hill, but always downwards, they eventually came across a typical rural dwelling - a small house which had two smaller outhouses, embraced by a walled courtyard, that was situated in a clearing. They cautiously approached the house, and the frail form of an elderly woman appeared at the doorway. Davies and Blackwell, having picked up a smattering of the language, indicated to her that they had a sick friend in grave need of water and nourishment. At this, the old woman called to someone inside the house, whereupon an elderly Korean man appeared, who greeted them in a friendly manner, much to their relief.

There followed a dialogue between the two Koreans before they indicated that the four soldiers should enter the house quickly. Once inside, they generously provided boiled rice and spiced vegetables. Never was food better-tasting or more appreciated, for they were ravenous. After the meal, the old man invited them to remain until Ron Allum had regained his walking-legs. That night they slept contentedly on their full stomachs. Yet, not forgetting the need to take it in turn to keep a watchful eye on the outside world.

About noon of the third day, the situation changed suddenly and dramatically when the old woman appeared before them distraught and in tears. It seemed that her grandson, only twelve years of age, had observed the men moving about the house and had dashed home to report this to his father. Realizing the peril this now placed their Korean benefactors in, they made preparations for a hasty departure. Regrettably, as they expressed their heartfelt gratitude to the Korean couple, the boy and his father appeared, armed with rifles.

The four were made to stand in line on the veranda. After a moment's deliberation, the man indicated that the party should move off. Tony Eagles suggested to Blackwell that they should disarm the man and boy, for they appeared to be quiet novice in their manner of handling the rifles. But, before this could happen, a burst of sub-machine-gun fire passed over their heads, as a Chinese soldier accompanied by a dozen North Korean policemen raced towards them.

They were marched off to the nearest village, where Ron Allum, still obviously ill, was taken away by a Chinese soldier to his headquarters, leaving the others to the mercy of the NKP. Their reputation for cruelty to British and Allied prisoners-of-war, especially those recaptured following escape attempts, is a matter of painful record by surviving British POWs.

The NKP lost no time in showing their true colours and cowardly ways. The escapees' wrists were bound with electric flex, then they were made to squat on their haunches with their backs to the police station wall. One NKP, who appeared to be in charge, lit a cigarette and offered it to Tony Eagles. He raised his head in acceptance of it, not expecting the NKP to reverse the cigarette at the last moment and then press the burning end against Tony's lips, but he did! Involuntarily, he spat in the policeman's face. He knew that his mother would have disapproved!

Pain embraced his mind and body with its ugly sensation as another NKP smashed the butt of his rifle into the Drummer's thigh with such brute force that Tony feared he had sustained a fracture from it. He was to discover afterwards that a cigarette case had taken some of the sting out of the blow. The badly-dented cigarette case is still in his possession to-day.

Eventually, they were taken to a shed at the rear of the police station, and again made to adopt the squat position. An armed guard remained in the room with them. Some time later, a middle-aged male civilian appeared at the door with a stick some 3 feet long and 1½ inches thick, which he proceeded to beat about the head and shoulders of the unfortunate Tony Eagles in a frenzied attack; his eyes full of loathing for the Englishman. Though some of the blows were dodged, it was not possible to avoid all of them from the squat position and with hands trussed.

There is a contained voilence in everyone, even in those who choose not to live by the rule of violence, and under severe provocation even they can be forced to react in a manner which, otherwise, would be alien to their nature.

Tony feared the man was demented and would eventually beat him to death. With this thought foremost in his mind, he lashed out with all his strength and his right foot sank deep into the man's groin. Though it put an end to the beating, Tony feared the price he would have to pay for protecting his own life: a life for a life, perhaps? However, the guard simply assisted the injured civilian to his feet and unceremoniously shoved him out of the shed. It was then that the guard told the battered Tony Eagles that the Korean's home had been destroyed in a bombing attack by one of our aircraft. He lost his entire family - wife, son, daughter-in-law and four grandchildren!

Soon after this incident, a man entered the shed wearing the self-effacing air of a small-time official, given something important to do for a change, who gestured to Blackwell to go outside. Several minutes passed before they heard angry voices, including Blackwell's, making rude comments about the North Korean Leader, Kim Il Sung. There were a number of pistol shots, followed by a prolonged silence. Davies and Eagles were too stunned by this development to speak to each other; all they could do was to exchange the facial expressions of their despair and shock. Not unnaturally so, they believed that Blackwell had been murdered by the merciless NKP.

The petty official re-entered the shed and fingered Davies to follow him. He turned to his friend and said:"I haven't known you long, Tony, but I have enjoyed your companionship. Whatever the outcome...see you somewhere...sometime." Moments later, more shots were fired. Tony Eagles thought: my turn next. They're both dead. His equanimity dispersed by the prospect.

One can imagine but never really know the feelings of his distress and utter desolation knowing that he was next to die. Feelings that were confused and disjointed by a redundance of thoughts and half-completed thoughts, each striving for his attention, before it was too late. Then his bodily functions all went to hell, leaving him with a terrible compulsion to evacuate his bowels all over the shed floor. And how futile it all seemed to the young Drummer having to ask the guard if he could go to the latrine - with only minutes to live!

Sitting on the box, he observed two NKP walk over to a hole-in-the-ground and commence discharging firearms into the hole. Christ, he thought, they really wanted to make sure that 'Blackie' and 'Davey' were dead! Then he heard the voices of his friends seeming to come out of the hole; cursing the two NKP in rich Anglo-Saxon rhetoric. The sadist policemen were playing a deadly game with the Americans - a variation of Russian roulette - firing bullets into the pit so that they ricocheted around the walls! He feared they would not survive long.

From the latrine, he was escorted back to the shed and, shortly afterwards, when leaving the shed again, a NKP snarled in broken English: "You Americans are criminals and do not deserve to live!" As an Englishman, he was not indifferent to being called an American. Though his companions were sterling people, he felt a compelling need to put the record straight, so he shouted into the face of the Korean: "If you are going to kill me, you should know that I am a British soldier!" The policeman turned to the other NKP and spoke before addressing further comment to Tony Eagles:"If you are indeed a British soldier, it will make a difference." (The enemy, particulary North Koreans, had a consuming hatred for all Americans.) He was then escorted back to the shed just as a platoon of Chinese soldiers arrived on the scene; no doubt to investigate what all the shooting was about. They marched the three prisoners off to their headquarters, where they were re-united with the sick Ron Allum; given food, which consisted of a chapati-like pancake stuffed with beanshoots, that was both pleasant and satisfying.

That night, they were marched away to the next destination. After several hours of non-stop marching, Ron Allum decided that he could go no further, knowing the intimidating consequences of such a decision - for they would shoot him; so Tony Eagles draped the weary body of his friend across his shoulders, sack-like, half-carrying and half-dragging him along. Though the Drummer was a strong young man, the effort soon exhausted him. His body began to feel itchy all over and sweat poured out of his body. When he glanced upwards at the moon he was reassured that it was large and bright as ever, though somewhat disconcerted by its colour - it was now bright green! Shortly afterwards, he passed into unconsciousness. And when he regained his senses, he discovered that 'Blackie' and 'Davey' were stretchering him, but without the benefit of a stretcher. The enemy never hesitated long before shooting any prisoner who failed to keep up the pace. Poor Ron Allum was left to cope on his own!

Several days had gone by when they entered a village occupied entirely by Chinese soldiers. Their escort handed the prisoners over to the senior officer in charge - a man with terrible facial scars that might well have been caused by napalm. He was to be their interrogator! And that process began by separating the four from each other. They were not to see one another again until the ordeal of interrogation by 'Scarface' was finished.

Drummer Eagles was taken into a courtyard where 'Scarface' was waiting; a Luger pistol gripped in one hand. He indicated to the Drummer that he was to sit on a boulder. A ritual that had taken place all too many times, decided the Englishman. "You are the ring leader who organized this escape," 'Scarface' said; so Tony

Eagles resorted to the pre-escape story they had agreed upon. After all, he logically concluded, Ron Allum was still a very sick man, and this would give credibility to the story, he thought. But there was something about the demeanor of 'Scarface' that forewarned him: no matter what was said, 'Scarface' would not be denied the torment that was to follow.

With the Luger now pointed directly at the Drummer, the Chinese Officer again said, "You are the ringleader", so Tony Eagles repeated his story. 'Scarface's' response was to order another Chinese soldier to step forward. This man had a British army issue.38 revolver in his hand. He raised it in front of the prisoner's eyes and inserted a single bullet into an otherwise empty cartridge-chamber; non -chalantly spinning the chamber before placing the barrel of the gun against his temple. 'Scarface' then repeated the question, and Tony Eagles denied it. A nod from 'Scarface' and the soldier squeezed the trigger!

The noise of the hammer striking the empty chamber reverberated along the barrel and into his brain. There was no comfort derived from his knowledge of small arms: that the weight of a single bullet ought to ensure that the cartridge-chamber, when spun, would come to rest with the bullet towards the bottom - away from where the hammer would have sent the bullet exploding into his brain. But, of course, there was no way of knowing if the revolver had been maintained in good working condition; and the prospect that it had not, filled Tony Eagles with anxiety.

The soldier then crossed over to the other side of the prisoner, spun the cartridge - chamber, and pressed the gun-barrel to Tony's temple. When the question was repeated and the same reply received, a nod from 'Scarface' signalled the soldier to squeeze the trigger. This time, though, the sound had a different quality to it, and this increased his fear: what if the bullet did not always settle in a position below the hammer? After all, history was full of men who had been killed playing the deadly game of Russian roulette.

When 'Scarface' once more asked the question, Tony Eagles hesitated momentarily before denying it, and in that split-second of time knew that the struggle was over for the Englishman. When the enemy soldier again squeezed the trigger Tony Eagles was sure that he detected the trigger being squeezed before the cartridge-chamber had come to a full stop. This lengthening provocation of his ordeal became intolerable. When the officer repeated the question, yet again, and the soldier spun in anticipation of a negative reponse from the Drummer, Tony Eagles decided that enough was enough.

"Yes, if you must insist," he said, "I am the leader."

And even as the words were leaving his lips he was filled with a deep sense of guilt and shame at his failure; consoling himself with the thought that he could do more good alive that dead; albeit, he had yet to survive the punishment they would inflict now that he had confessed. If they didn't get you one way, they would certainly get you in another way.

Blackwell and Davies were sentenced to 28 days imprisonment in the 'hole,' because it was their second escape attempt. Ron Allum and Tony Eagles jointly received 14 days in the 'hole.' This, quite simply, was a hole-in-the-ground with a cover of sorts placed over it so that no light could penetrate. To answer a call-of-nature, one had to crawl out from under this. On one such visit to the latrine, a sentry dropped a few leaves of tobacco near at hand, in a rare gesture of human kindness. The grateful British soldiers made roll-ups using the pages of the New Testament which had been left together with a cigarette lighter when they were thrown into the 'hole;' helping to make the 14 days subterranean punishment less disagreeable.

Of the warm-hearted Korean couple, who had extended the milk of human kindness to four desperately hungry Allied soldiers, Tony Eagles would like to think that they had escaped any punishment, by virtue of their age. But knowing the North Korean police mentality, coupled with the nature of their 'crime,' he feels it would be stretching the imagination too far not to expect them to have been punished. But wherever they are - in this life or the hereafter - he feels sure that they will remember the four soldiers for their gratitude. For their courage and for their kindness, Tony Eagles will remember them, always.

A year or more following the escape bid, Tony Eagles and Davies met up in the prison camp hospital. Tony learned that his other friend, 'Blackie,' had died from pheumonia within months of their recapture. There is much to remember his American comrades for: most of all, he remembers them for their courage and their fortitude and their indomitable spirit and for saving his life when they 'stretchered' his unconscious body, shortly after re-capture. And of 'Davey,' who knows whether or not he survived the prisoner of war camps!

Chapter 9

DENIS WOODS' WAR

By Ashley Cunningham-Boothe

Invite Denis Woods for a reason why he fought in Korea and most likely he will reply: "Because I was born out of time!" Yet, as a young soldier in the Korean War his mind never sought an explanation of what he was doing there. To-day he offers, by way of explanation, the following. Like countless others, he was first ordered to attend a centre for the mandatory medical examination that would determine his fitness to serve as a conscript in the army. This was a process millions knew from personal experience as fundamental and expeditious - a procedure born out of the urgency of wartime - which involved checking a man's vital organs for evidence that all worked well, before issuing a buff card of officialdom and of approbation: proclaiming his fitness to fight for his country.

Following this statutory and perfunctory examination of the human anatomy - consisting of the essential "Cough and bend over, lad", - Denis Woods was informed that he was A1 : fit for duty in the Infantry! And the fact that he desperately wanted to serve as an infantry soldier helped to reconcile the differences of opinion regarding his eyesight. One is tempted to say that he "turned a blind eye" to an impediment in his right eye, which had left him almost blind since childhood, so that he could serve his King and Country as a soldier.

"Being the very worse kind of snob," as he puts it, "A valley-born Welsh snob," he elected to serve in that most famous of Welsh Regiments - The South Wales Borderers. Within the first week of commencing his training in the Training Battalion at Brecon, however, he was transfered to the equally famous Welch Regiment, so named; thus learning out of that experience the first valuable lesson in understanding army life: choice of a personal nature is denied the ordinary mortal. He does as he is told. His personal wishes are of no concern to the military establishment.

The disciplines of basic training and the rituals of army life (never to be forgotten by all initiates) were accommodated with comparative ease by our intrepid 'Rookie,' who had learned much of the routine as a cadet back in his home town of Tonypandy.

Part way through the basic training programme it was discovered that he could only operate a Bren-gun left-handed. This was so that he could engage his one good eye for sighting the weapon. But firing a Bren-gun from the left shoulder can be a precarious business, as those familiar with the mechanics of this weapon will testify, because of the manner in which spent cartridge-cases are ejected from the gun. However, notwithstanding the nature of his disability, 'Rookie' Woods had qualified on such small arms as the Sten gun and the rifle as well as the Bren-gun, and with consistently high-score results. This fact seemed to have little persuasive appeal to the range officer, who discovered Private Woods firing a Bren-gun from his left sholder, and was mortified at the sight of the cumbersome skill that this involved. The young soldier was challenged for an explanation for the need for his 'caggy-handed' technique with the Bren-gun.

After listening to the 'Rookie' soldier's explanation, the range officer proclaimed "with the pompous air of authority and of someone wanting to moralize over a particular point of view," claims Denis Woods, "Ah, well... now let's see you try your hand at firing a PIAT!" The PIAT (Projectile Infantry Anti-Tank) resisted all attempts by the young soldier with his impediment and 'caggy-handed' technique, reminding the now mature Denis Woods of Robert G. Ingersoll's famous remark: "There are in nature neither rewards nor punishments - there are consequences." So the awful truth of his ophthalmic impediment became a matter for official records, proving to be the downfall of his ambition to serve in the Army as an infantry soldier. In truth, he had become an embarrassment to the military establishment. He was tagged a 'one-eyed Jack' and sent to Maindy Barracks to have his eyes tested properly, this time.

The Optician expressed his amazement that Private Woods had been accepted for service in the Army - especially in the Infantry - with such poor vision in his right eye that he was almost blind. And when the army-issue spectacles were issued some days later, he tried them for fit and cosmetic affect (in private, of course) and then vowed never to be seen in public wearing them.

Within a few days of being issued with his glasses, he was ordered to pack his kitbag and report to the guardroom where transport was to convey him to another Regiment - just like that! - where his lack of optical excellence, so he was told, would not be such a matter of grave concern to everyone!

Arriving at his new Regiment - The Royal Artillery - he found himself redesignated "Gunner." However, Gunner in title was all that the Royal Artillery were going to permit him, for they took the pragmatic view that no 'one-eyed Jack' could ever be a Gunner, then promptly sent him off for training as a Signaller. This did not stop the intrepid Gunner Woods from consistently qualifying as a marksman on small arms each passing year, and with a determination to show his colleagues and the establishment that he could out-shoot many of his comrades with Bisley marksmanship. Qualifying as a Signaller on the basic course, he was then made to attend an advanced students course, which he passed, leading to his promotion as a Lance-Bombadier Signaller Instructor.

It was about this time in his military career that he felt he had been born out of time. The origin for this feeling was that he really wanted to be a British Redcoat soldier - "Men of honour" and "Men of glory," to quote Denis - in the great days of the British Empire, when such men were understandably proud of having been "A serving of Her Majesty The Queen," relating extraordinary tales of valour in the field to enthralled audiences. He wished, too, that he had been a part of that time in British history when men stood side by side in "The Thin Red Line," or shoulder to shoulder in "The Hollowed Square", and regretted not having had the opportunity in life to brace himself, as they had done, against a resolute enemy because, as he says: "Being born a hundred years too late!"

When Communist Forces from North Korea invaded South Korea in June of 1950 (considered by most people in Britain at the time to be "at the other end of the earth!") he saw this heaven-sent opportunity for someone, like himself, "Born out of time," to volunteer for active duty and face the challenge in a now-or-never chance to brace himself against an enemy on the field of conflict as the "Redcoats" had done. Not so much with "shades of Empire" or the proud rattling of sabres, but that ancient call to arms that always attracts eager young men.

Nowadays, if he is pressed and needs must, he will explain it as simply satisfying a deep-seated need to be a soldier and to fight any fight in all its magnificent glory. He sees it all summed up in Henry Ward Beecher's insight: "It is not merely cruelty that leads men to war, it is excitment." When he read in one of the national newspapers of a major battle (the Naktong River) involving British troops, which had resulted in large numbers of casualties being suffered and many being taken prisoners of war, he immediately applied for a regular engagment (only those on such engagments and over the age of nineteen years were permitted to serve in Korea in the early months of the war). This completed and his 'King's Shilling' well and truly spent, followed by two weeks embarkation leave and a brief spell at Woolwich Barracks, he took his place aboard a troopship at Liverpool docks bound for "The Land of the Morning Calm."

Among those aboard the troopship were two World War Two veterans - Army Reservists recalled to the Colours - and not exactly enthralled at the prospect of fighting another war and with a 'one-eyed Jack' of a Lance-Bombardier, whom they promised to devour for breakfast, the way old soldiers do. In weeks that it took to reach Pusan, Denis Woods learned much from the two Reservists. As an Observation Post Signaller, he was called upon to do his fair share of patrols attached to a famous infantry regiment. Yet, still the thirst for action remained unsatisfied. Where was the 'Hollow Square'? and where was the "Thin Red Line"? Real soldiers did not fight from holes in the ground!

In his youth, he had been brought up on a diet of mass-produced Hollywood war movies, on books and poems and epics which glorified the deeds of war, brainwashed - like many of his generation - by the scriptwriters' propaganda and the skills of John Ford and Cecil B. de Mille and their like. Now Korea brought home the awful reality of the false impressions of war created to sell books and films. He learned, for example, that bullets fired in his direction did not seem at all like sounds created by Hollywood sound effects engineers, but sounded much more aggressive, like swarms of angry bees. That the bodies of the newly-dead were rubbery until stiffened by rigor mortis. Nothing like so much as the dead in John Wayne and Errol Flynn war movies.

Part of the essential learning process at the 'sharp end' was discovering that war is nine-tenths boredom, waiting for something to happen in. He learned fast the habit of sleeping with one watching-eye squinting at every suspicious movement; his ears cocked for each sound that was different. He acquired a taste for combat rations and actually enjoyed them! He learned the unpalatable truth, sad that it was, and regardless of the fact we spoke a common language, that there was little mutual understanding and communication between Americans and Britons, mainly due to the competitve spirit of both nationalities, except in the case of the individual Yank and Tommy, who got on well with each other.

Much of the survival experience for the frontline soldier depends upon a variety of purpose-built holes in the ground, and he learned to dig each one of them (hence the vulgar endearment "The Shitdiggers," which infantry soldiers call each other): hole to sleep in, holes to fight in, holes to hide away in, holes to escape in, holes to defecate in, holes for mortars and machine-guns, holes for mines and booby-traps and holes to bury your friends in! Each hole having its own authenticity of purpose and its own distinguishing name; no two being alike.

He learned, also, the skill in survival and living with other creatures trying to survive on him and others - rats, centipedes, snakes, leeches and creepy-crawlies of every kind as well as the ever present and persistent flies and mosquitoes. Learning the awful necessity of survival in the extremes of climate - the scorching heat of sub-tropical summers and the killer-cold of the sub-artic winters - was an experience that would stay in his mind for ever, and nothing would cloud the images of recollection. In between these seasons of discomfort (with water rationed to a pint per man per day) he learned to survive in the torrential downpourings that accompanied the monsoon season, which seemed to go on for ever and ever. And in contrast to this, during the dry season, surviving the pervading clouds of ochre-coloured dust that blanketed the entire landscape and everything upon it.

He learned to tolerate, albeit reluctantly, the perverse stench that offended the senses of everyone. This rose from the rice fields that were covered with human excreta, which had been ladled out of army field latrines by unfortunate young women, who were thus disfavoured with the stigma "shit-biddy," by the British Tommy.

He became self-reliant, and learned to trust his intuition on important matters, often made in great haste whenever the unexpected occurred or during enemy attack. He studied with growing curiosity the old and the young soldiers who employed deception and guile in their day-to-day juggling with circumstances so that they appeared to officers and NCOs as being nothing more than ordinary or unobtrusive, this was in the hope that they would not be called upon to perform some act or duty that would escalate them among the ranks of the extraordinary, where many were destined, anyway. Observing, also, the young men who, like himself, had arrived in Korea inexperienced at warfare, grow into campaign veterans quickly.

He remembers those who performed deeds of outstanding conduct or of courage and how, all too often, such deeds went unrewarded, because those whose rank matters in such things had not been spectators at the time; as well as those who opened their hearts in the privacy of comradeship to proclaim inner fears and dread of battle, yet, overcame such fears when the time came as, indeed, must all those who wear the soldier's uniform, if they want to avoid the company of cowards.

All this, he was reminded frequently by the two Reservists who coached him in the business of war, was part and parcel of what Denis Woods had come to Korea for - death and glory! Yet, even by the time he had completed his tour of duty in Korea and was then shipped to another overseas posting, where he quickly grew disenchanted with the boring predictability of peacetime soldiering, his thirst for eyeball-to-eyeball confrontation with the enemy remained unquenched.

His attempt to enlist in La Légion Etrangère was disapproved of by the military establishment. They were, after all, still paying him the coin of the realm for the unexpired portion of his regular engagement. So he vounteered for duty with the Special Air Service in Malaya, and was excited by being placed on their waiting list. Of course, the trouble with wanting to belong to an élite fighting unit is the long list of waiting volunteers, which can seem to be endless when you are in a hurry. Eventually, he found himself in the position of having insufficient service remaining to make training with the SAS worthwhile; so he then volunteered for a second tour in Korea and was posted to 20th Field Regiment RA, which was earmarked to replace 14th Field Regiment RA in Korea which had, in its time, relieved his original regiment - 45th Field Regiment RA.

The highlight of this 'second bite of the cherry' was his involvement in a history making action which, eventually, transpired to be the last major battle fought anywhere in the world by British troops, until the Falklands Campaign some three decades later. It was fought on a notorious piece of Korean landscape called "The Hook," which will long be remembered by those who fought for it. And it was here that Denis Woods, the 'one-eyed Jack' of a gunner, gratified the ancient call to arms and tasted the excitement of battle, just as yesterdays' soldiers had in the "Hollowed Square" and in the "Thin Red Line".

On that notorious hill in Korea, called "The Hook", the 'Rookie' became a veteran, writing the pages of history.

Chapter 10

UNIDENTIFIED FLYING OBJECT

By Major General P. A. Downward, CB, DSO, DFC

Having filed my flight-plan in Operations at "Dragon Base", otherwise Headquarters 8th Army Air Strip on Seoul racecourse, I collected my helmet and gloves from the crew room and left the warm smoky atmosphere for the aircraft dispersal a few yards away to find my beloved Auster Mk VI. The American ground crew had already removed the control locks from the wings and the tail, and I was delighted to see that someone had had the good sense to put the trunk of the hot air blower into the cockpit in addition to a second trunk into the engine cowling. At least I should be reasonably certain of a good start. Although tempted to get into the pilot's seat and get out of the cold, I meticulously checked the outside of the aircraft, turned the prop a couple of times by hand, kicked the tyres, checked the buckles on the cowlings and wiggled the ailerons, rudder and elevators, at the same time ensuring that all snow and frost had been removed from the skin. She was clean even though one couldn't say she was pristine; at least I knew the airframe was complete, and to all outward appearances - airworthy.

Being a very cold day with the outside temperature several degrees below freezing, I gave the engine a long run up before going through the pre-flight checks, finally checking the freedom of the controls, and then with a wave to the ground-crew to clear the chocks I taxied out to the end of the strip which, in better days, must have been the four furlong straight down to the winning post. A final run-up against the brakes and then I was bumping over the frozen surface, quickly gathering speed, to become airborne about half way along the strip.

One pleasant aspect of flying over Korea in winter months was the tremendous visibility in the cold air, and also a lack of turbulence except if it were windy. This day was smooth, and on passing over Uijongbu in my flight northwards to "Fort George",where 1913 Light Liaison Flight R.A.F. was based, I decided to let down and do a bit of tactical low flying through the valleys in the rear area of the Division. I could identify clearly the familiar land marks, the Ordnance Field Park, the Field Pay Office, the fuel dumps and ammo dumps, and everywhere along the frozen roads the constant scurry of Army vehicles. My attention perhaps was not entirely on my flying, ambulances were obvious and one felt for the poor devils inside as I knew that there had been a heavy assault on the "Hook" the night before. A Korean family with their white baggy clothing, and menfolk carrying loaded 'A' frames shot underneath me, and then I entered a narrow valley which dictated that I kept my eyes up in case some other harebrain was low-flying in the other direction. It was very much a one-way street round the back of the mountain Kamaksan with not very much outlet to the starboard side where there was a steep rocky slope, and only a marginally better outlet on the port side.

A few hundred yards from the end of the valley, just as I was looking ahead for the familiar land-mark of the Imjin River I felt a slight bump and looked to both main planes to see if I had perhaps hit a bird. Nothing! I thought no more about it and

Pilots and Auster aircraft of 1913 Light Liaison Flight, 1953. From left to right: S/Sgt. Rolley, Capt. P. F. Wilson, Capt. H. Irwin, D.F.C., Sgt. Cameron, Capt. P. A. Downward, D.F.C., S/Sgt. Hall, Lt. J. Shaw, Sgt. Hutchings, D.F.M. They wear the red berets of the Glider Pilot Regiment.

An Auster spotter plane of 1903 A.O.P. Flight, taken by Gunner R. Barton, 42 Mortar Battery.

immediately became interested in the building of a NAAFI/EFI roadhouse going up at the side of the road at the junction leading up towards Pintail bridge. With the thought of the previous night's action in mind, I flew northwards over the Imjin in order to have a look at the forward area keeping a sharp lookout for a platoon of 3-inch mortars that had given me a fright a couple of days before. Listening to the Gunner net on the 62 set, I could hear that a target was being engaged somewhere to the right and ahead of me, by 25 pounders of 16 Regiment RNZA. Whilst I still had enough turning room before having to go under their trajectories, I headed back for home to the Commonwealth strip alongside the Imjin. With a green light from the control point (you couldn't call it a tower), I landed in the best Middle Wallop style, quickly taxied to my dispersal and turned the aircraft round so that she was ready for lifting straight back under the camouflage net, tail first.

In the crew room, the name given to the rather untidy structure round the command post, I signed up the Authorization Book and the Aircraft 700, and seized a cup of indifferent but warming coffee from the pot on the space heater. Whilst contemplating the Marilyn Monroe calendar on the notice board, I was summond by SAC Gorringe, the Airman in charge of my aircraft, to come and have a look at VF547 as somehow or other I had sustained some damage to the tail. I had to confess, I had not checked the aircraft after landing, and was certain that nothing had come up from the runway in taking off or landing in my last trip. But there, sure enough, was a wapping great hole in my tail plain on the starboard side. Flight Sergeant Carr, the senior RAF technician looked distinctly displeased as he was certain that someone had mishandled the aircraft on the ground - not the pilot, of course! After a few minutes detective work by the accepted experts, the airframe mechanics, it was decided categorically that the missile must have come from above the aircraft unless, of course, I had been flying upside down! A most unlikely venture in an Auster, particularly when low-flying. With further keen detective work it was decided that it could not have been a 3-inch mortar bomb or a 25 pounder shell, or surely I would have noticed! I agreed readily. Had I been over the enemy line where there was an open season for shooting at aircraft? I then remembered my possible bird-strike somewhere over Gloucester Valley, but this gash on the tail could not possibly have been caused by a bird. It was quite obviously a missile, and no matter whether it was from the enemy side of the line or ours, it was considered a most unfriendly act on somebody's part; and with that the ground crew set to work repairing it.

Less than an hour after the repair had been made to the tail plane, and while the paint was still drying, the Flight Sergeant appeared in the command post with a grin on his face, or what I could see of it under the hood of his parka jacket. "I think we've found the answer to your flak damage, Sir!" he remarked, and led me outside to the dispersal where I saw a Canadian Brigade jeep, and standing beside it a very worried looking Captain of the Royal Canadian Engineers. I knew him by sight as I had often seen him around the area with his troop repairing the roads and culverts, and remembered that he had helped us out with resurfacing the airstrip in the wet weather. I greeted him with some inanity like "nice to see you again", which immediately evoked the response "I'm not here on a social visit!" He explained that he had come hot-foot from the Rear Divisional area in order to find me, the Flight Commander, and muttered something about a Board of Enquiry. It was obvious he was trying to get his word in first on some small drama.

The Captain explained that his Troop had been working in the Rear Divisional area, close to the side of Kamaksan where they had recently made a quarry in the outcrop of rock so as to build up a reserve of crushed stone for their road works. They had dislodged about a couple of hundred tons of rock that morning, and were doing one final blasting before calling it a day. He had taken all the proper precautions, once the explosive charges had been set. The lookouts had ensured that none of the local populace were in the area, the road was closed five hundred yards either side of the quarry entrance, and with a final warning of "blasting now" over his loud hailer, he pressed the plunger on the magneto and up went another fifty tons of rock. "But how the hell was I to know that one of your god-damned pilots was going to come swanning up the valley in his puddle-jumper just in the middle of my blasting?" Naturally, I expressed surprise, I suppose I could say I was genuinely staggered at the thought of flying through a shower of turnip sized rocks returning to earth from about three or four hundred feet. "There was absolutely nothing I could do but pray" he added. I could see no trace of such supplication on the knees of his trousers, nevertheless, I thanked him for his kind thought, and after a few questions as to how close to disaster the pilot had been, I discontinued my enquiries and assured him that one of our aircraft had suffered a bit of superficial damage, but had returned safely to base. There was no question of a Board of Enquiry. I would speak to the pilot straight away; "He should certainly have known better!" I thanked the Captain profusely for his concern and saw him to his jeep. More than ever, I was aware of Flight Sergeant Carr's grin from under the hood of his parka jacket. Flak indeed!

Chapter 11

OF RATS AND MEN

By Ron Larby

I arrived in Korea during November, 1951, serving with a Royal Signals Troop which was attached to the 14th. Field Regiment Royal Artillery. When the morning of disembarkation arrived, our curiosity drove us to ship's muster with much more enthusiasm than on previous occasions. First of all, we noticed the hospital mercy ship moored alongside, reminding us of the stark reality of our purpose in being at the other end of the world... where one could get hurt if not, indeed, killed! The American, all-negro military band belting out 'The Saint Louis Blues March!', seemed quite inappropriate, failing miserably to disguise the sombre feelings deep inside of each of us; for we had come for a fight!

At Pusan, we entrained at a time which coincided with the arrival of a Red Cross hospital train from the forward battle areas. Less severely wounded American GIs - the walking wounded - ear-balled us, knowing that we had just arrived and that we were as green as God's little apples between spring and summer: "Your turn next, buddies!" Yet another reminder that we had come a long way to do a dirty and difficult job and, perhaps, for some of us, it could mean that we might well remain for ever in The Land of the Morning Calm or, at best, discover the experience to be a painful one.

The Officer Commanding 14th. Field Royal Artillery preferred to drive his own jeep. I recall, too, that he usually managed to get his radio headset and his microphone mixed - he would speak into the headset and listen with the microphone! His radio operator was a Signaller Payne, and it was he who recounted the following narrative, which happened shortly after our arrival in Korea.

Driving past a United States Army Artillery Battery, the CO, in the driving seat as usual, singled out the guns to Signaller Payne with outstretched arm and pointed a finger: "That one's a 105", then changed his mind: "No! it's a 155" almost as quickly again, changed his mind: "Or, are they 105's?"

Seeing an American GI lounging nearby, helmet at the droop and almost covering his eyes; hands up to his elbows inside his GI issue dungarees; his mouth with slow and deliberate movements chewing the all-American chewing-gum; the CO pulled the jeep to a stop within talking distance of the GI and politely greeted him accordingly:
"Good morning!"
"Mawnen!" responded the Yank in a deep southern drawl.
"Those guns over there, are they 105s or 155s?"
Mustering the energy to extract one hand from the sanctuary of his dungarees pocket, he tipped the helmet towards the back of his head, studied the guns for a moment or two then turned to reply to the question put to him.
"Goddamned if I know! I only got heah maself this mawnen!"
...Oh, how great are the number of innocents abroad in times of war!

Shortly before Christmas 1951, I was transferred to 28 Commonwealth Brigade, where I met up with a Driver David 'Lord' Kitchener. He was to accompany me when I was posted to the King's Shropshire Light Infantry. 'Lord' Kitchener's political conviction was not exactly what one might have expected from a British 'Squaddie' on active service in Korea to fight a Communist aggressor, for he was a self-professed and ardent Communist! He spent hours endeavouring to persuade the Korean mess-bods that life, for them, would be infinitely better under Communist government. What strange bedmates war makes of us all!

Everyone knew of 'Lord' Kitchener's political convictions, yet, I don't believe for one moment that any of us took him seriously; at the most... just taking the piss out of him! I recall, for example, during the Christmas celebrations, Brigadier 'Long John' MacDonald, upon seeing David 'Lord' Kitchener, calling out to him: "Good heavens, Kitchener, should you not be celebrating on the other side?"

On a more serious note: one of the annoying problems which we endured, particularly during 1952, when the frontline had become a fixed line of hillside trenches and dugouts, was a plague of rats. Life became as much a nightmare from these horrible creatures as from mortar bombs. They seemed to be as large as cats, especially in the dark. No part of the entrenchments escaped their curiosity. It seemed to us at the time that every damned rat in Korea was on our accommodation and rations list. I should not have been at all surprised if the whole rodent community was ensconced in the position occupied by the Royal Signals Rear Link Attachment with the 1st Battalion The King's Shropshire Light Infantry!

Finally, Kitchener and I decided on a plan to rid ourselves of the rats. Using the fumes from a chore-horse - this is a battery-charging machine - we devised an ingenious scheme to gas the overfed rodents by stationing the chore-horse inside the radio bunker, then blocking-up the entrance, so that the fumes given off would eventually penetrate the rat holes and, hopefully, kill them. After arranging the headsets so as to permit us to operate the radios from outside of the bunker, the chore-horse was put into operation and left to run inside the bunker. We sat back with the curiosity of those with too much time on their hands to await the result of our ingenious anti-rat plan.

After about twenty minutes, the chore-horse was turned off, and the obstruction we had erected to block-off the entrance to the radio was then removed. Being a considerable way up the side of a mountain, reaching half way to heaven, I suppose one could be forgiven if one expected the wind to blow clean the air inside the bunker in no time at all. In point of fact, it took hours for the fumes to clear altogether, not only from the radio bunker but from the tunnels and rat holes which led off the bunker.

It was a truly amazing sight to see the great number of stupified rats eventually staggering out of the radio bunker; being assisted with ruthless efficiency and a British Tommy's size 9 ammo boots on the road to extinction; some being bayonet-lifted by Kitchener and myself onto the flames of our brewing-up fire. Not many survived. Knowing what a nation of animal lovers we British are supposed to be in the eyes of the rest of the world, I have often wondered what folks would have thought of us at home had they been able to see the slaughter of the rodents.

In the summer of 1952, I spent some of my time working as a radio operator to the Brigade Major. During my time at brigade headquarters, a new Brigade Major was appointed, and he took the earliest opportunity to visit all the Brigade positions and units. One such visit took him to the positions held by our Commonwealth cousins, the Australians; the outgoing Brigade Major accompanying us on this occasion. Though dress in the frontline is very much a casual business - one of the few perks of soldiering in the frontline - the Aussie infantry soldier seemed to me to be the more outrageous of non-dressers.

As we approached the headquarters of the 3rd Bn. The Royal Australian Regiment, one of their numbers was striding a well-worn footway attired only in his cellular drawers; his shirt and trousers over one arm and his other arm was seen to be supporting a revolver, holster and belt; his bush hat worn at a rakish angle; his gait the jaunty carriage of confidence we had come to expect from our Australian comrades. The incoming Brigade Major cast a disapproving eye towards the Australian. The outgoing Brigade Major caught this look and said to the new man: "One of the better dressed Australians I fear". And when the Australian threw out a cheerful greeting - "Godday to yer mates! How are yer?" - flapping an armful of uniform, which was the next best thing to a salute, the new boy's expression said it all. The outgoing B.M. acknowledged the salute, wearing an enormous grin.
"By the way, old boy," said the old B.M., "may I introduce you to the Adjutant!"

In the front-line bunkers and hoochies, the usual form of heating in winter was the "chuffer" stove, made from a metal ammunition box. Petrol dripped into it from a tube coming from a can high up outside. The whole thing was very primitive and it was easy to make a mistake with the highly inflammable petrol. The results in a small space, candle lit and sealed up for the warmth, could be disastrous. I remember one dreadful occasion when I saw a soldier running screaming from his bunker burning from head to foot. It is a memory which I can never forget.

Ron Larby in his 'better hole'.

Chapter 12

GEORGE MARTIN'S PUSAN TRAIN

By Ashley Cunningham-Boothe

In 1952, B Company 1st Bn. King's Shropshire Light Infantry was sent to Koje Island, off the south coast, to help the Americans to guard the huge P.O.W. camp. Soon afterwards, Sergeant 'Bomber' Wells took me aside and informed me that I was being posted to Koje Island as a replacement cook. At first, I thought he had said: "Coney Island", so I had visions of a trip to the United States of America! The glazed expression on my face was wiped clean as soon as I read my orders: Corporal Brightman and Private Martin to travel to Koje Island; travelling by train to Pusan. Furthermore, we were to take a jeep with us. Now...everyone knows that you cannot fit a jeep into a railway carriage - it simply cannot be done! However, orders are orders and, anyway, who were we to challenge the wisdom of the order-makers?

Dutifully, we reported to the railhead, which was situated some twenty miles from Seoul, where we discovered that our railway carriage was the fresh-air version - a flatcar - wide-open to the elements! In truth, there were no railway carriages on this particular train at all. Not only was there to be no shelter for Corporal Brightman and myself on the flatcar, but we were soon to discover that this train appeared to run to no particular timetable whatsoever!

Enquiring of a large, cigar-chewing American G.I., who was carrying a clipboard of officialdom, as to which of the flatcars was to be ours, he pointed his stubby finger in the direction of the most dilapidated piece of rolling-stock I had ever seen, filling me with great concern for our safety. Closer examination of the flatcar heightened our alarm, for large holes appeared all over the floor - large enough for my mate to have fallen through!

With some difficulty, we managed to get the jeep loaded and, this task completed, politely enquired of the clipboard-carrying G.I. "Noncom", "Koje Island?"

"Well now...that all depends upon Jeff Chandler and Humphry Bogart," came his laconic response. As is the endearing idiosyncrasy of servicemen of all nationalities - sticking nicknames on foreigners whose countries they occupied - it seemed not unreasonable that we should associate Chandler and Bogart as being nicknames for the Korean nationals who, as fireman and driver respectively, were responsible for jerking us all the way to Pusan.

After an interminable delay, the train moved off, shunting to and fro for about ten miles in either direction - as though it were vital for them to get their bearings first - before finally coming to rest near some large, hanger-like buildings.

"Youse guys wanna see Jeff Chandler?" How could we miss the opportunity of wringing the hand (or the neck) of the lunatic train-driver responsible for jerking us to and fro; so we jumped down from the flatcar and headed for the engine. "Not that way, Mac!" he full-lunged above the sound of the escaping engine steam. "The movie joint's this way, Mac."

One of the hanger-like buildings was a makeshift cinema. Showing on the screen was Jeff Chandler. So, the train had stopped merely to permit the American train personnel to "go watch a movie!"

After staying in the rail-siding all night - thank God not seeing Jeff Chandler all night - we set off again. During the overnight stay we had scrounged food to supplement the meagre rations provided by a niggardly Quartermaster. With the food, we also collected two copies of the American Forces newspaper "The Stars and Stripes." One copy was for reading (to keep up with the war news!), and the other copy for a much-needed personal use; using the holes in the flatcar as a sort of Japanese (no seat) lavatory; giving due allowance for wind pressure...! With true British ingenuity, we erected a shelter with items of personal belongings to protect us from the night's bitterly cold wind. Our groundsheets were positively invaluable!

Shortly after this stage of our journey to Pusan had begun, we noticed that, somehow, we had acquired a passenger in the jeep - a Korean boy of some twelve summers, we speculated. He was fast asleep in the back of the jeep. When he woke up, we addressed him in Pidgeon-Korean, asking of him: "Why are you on the train?"

"Me go Pusan!" which he repeated with determination in response to each of our questions; leaving us in no doubt that Pusan was where he was going...so we might as well get accustomed to the notion. Needless to say, we nicknamed him "Mego," and he served us well on the journey. Each time the train stopped, which was frequently - and, somehow, he always seemed to know which were the long stops and which were the short ones - he would disappear and return just before the train set off again; almost as though he had a timetable! More importantly, he always had items of food with him, which supplemented further the rations we were now sharing with him.

Next day, Brightman and I discovered that our numbers had increased by one. How he had got on to the train was as much a mystery to us as how Mego had managed it. But there he was, and the expression in his eyes said the same things: "Me go Pusan!"

"Him my brother," said Mego, as though to indemnify the newcomer's purpose. Thus, convinced by Mego that the other was family, we allowed him to stay. Well...it wasn't our train; and there was a war on! Two days later, our numbers had grown, yet again, by two small male persons; all looking the same age as Mego!

"Him and him brothers," said Mego, intending to cancel out any opposition by us to their being with us. We accepted Mego's instant family with the unquestioning fait accompli of soldiers at war.

With an increase to Mego's family of another two, the next day, it created problems of accommodation and food and clothing, for the kids were clothed in rags and were starving. Because the British soldier is renowned for his generosity to children - particularly to war-orphans - Brightman and I shared food, clothing and accommodation; albeit none of it was special.

That evening the train shunted jerkily into a siding; the engine was uncoupled and Mik and Kim, the engine-crew left the connected flatcars with its two British 'Squaddies' and instant-made Korean family to cope as best we could miles from signs of life.

Mego and mates drifted off silently and stealthily - like infantry soldiers on a night patrol - to forage for supplies. Brightman and I estimated that we had travelled about half the distance of the journey to Pusan. In that time we had seen three films and we had increased our limited vocabulary of the Korean language, thanks to Mego. We had learned the knack of making much out of nothing, feeding our instant family, which, in some ways, reminded me of the parable of Jesus and the loaves of bread and the fish.

All the next day we remained in the siding. Food nor water was on offer from any source. The boys did not forage during the hours of daylight, it was too dangerous. Korean Military Police had a reputation for brutality.

One of the boys, we discovered, was called Hego. Being so like Mego, we had not detected the difference until Mego himself laboured the nickname: "Hego...Hego...Hego!" anxiously and tersely; pointing his grubby finger in the direction of one of the boys. It seemed that Hego had been delegated, because of his fleetness and his success at avoiding capture by the ROK Military Police.

"Hego for chop-chop...bring rice." And he did! So, in this way, we were able to eke out the Compo rations supplied to us, for what was expected to be a quick jaunt down the road to Pusan but, instead, took the better part of eight days; with the begged and borrowed and stolen food which Hego and Mego and family had acquired for us.

The next day, by which time we were feeling some concern about our situation, a train with another Mik and Kim crew arrived. It seemed that the original Mik and Kim had been drafted onto more pressing war-work on a train-load of supplies for the forward area. However, they had overlooked the need to mention that two British soldiers were left behind on a flatcar; so there had been no urgency in providing the train with another engine and crew. It seemed that nobody knew about us, at all...!

By the time we eventually arrived at Pusan we had seen Howard Keel...live! And another movie. Before the train entered the restricted area of the Pusan railway station, Hego and the other boys had melted into the surrounding area. Mego refused to leave us. He became our cookhouse-boy after a lot of verbal exchanges with MPs and our own 'brass'. In fact, we had to keep Mego, for he was wearing a great deal of our G1098 kit. It seemed the only sure way of getting our clothes back!

When we finally drove the jeep ashore at Koje Island, where we were met by an irate Company Sergeant Major, we had a devil of a job convincing him that we really had taken eight days to do the journey. His response summed up much of the misunderstanding of that journey, when he said: "The next time I want a jeep transported here, I shall have it brought by bloody train!"

Chapter 13

LETTERS FROM SEOUL

By Gillian McNair

I - Jill Hall in those days - joined Queen Alexandra's Royal Army Nursing Corps as a Nursing Officer in November 1950 aged 23 years. After serving at Cambridge Military Hospital, Aldershot, I sailed in February 1952 on HMT *Empire Trooper* to Japan, to nurse at the British Commonwealth General Hospital, Kure. There I was a junior member of a team of Australian, Canadian, British nursing sisters and physiotherapists, one of some eighty women living in the busy base port, who with the R.A.M.C. nursed and cared for the large numbers of badly wounded and sick servicemen.

From 21st March - 26th April 1953, I was in charge of the small ambulance train, running from Iwakuni via Hiroshima to Kure, collecting the wounded from Korea, and also taking the convalescent patients to the airport for U.K. evacuation. I was also privileged to collect the first thirty British P.O.W.s to be released from Korea.

Until 1952 conditions in Korea were such, that no 'QA's were allowed to serve there (despite many requests) but in September, the first small Commonwealth hospital was formed in Seoul. Officially titled the Britcom Communication Zone Medical Unit, it was usually shortened to Britcom Z Medical Unit. Two 'QA's, two Australian and two Canadian Nursing Sisters were sent to serve the maximum of two months there. I was posted to Seoul in May 1953. Some time ago, I typed a version of my letters home with extra details added. Extracts from these follow.

Britcom Z Medical Unit B.A.P.O. 3.
Wednesday, 27 May, 1953.

At Iwakuni (Japan) we were driven out to the airstrip to our waiting plane. This turned out to be an old R.A.F. Dakota, which looked surprisingly small, somewhat tinny and quite unlike the luxurious Skymaster in which Cynthia and I flew to Tokyo last March. The interior of the Dakota was even more surprising to my unpractised feminine eye. Just a bare fuselage, with long canvas litters on each side of the plane to sit on and attached to these were canvas back rests and safety belts. I had an awful job to buckle my belt and I really felt too shy to ask one of the soldiers sitting next to me, especially because I was trying to look as though I really was on active service.

We took off at 5 a.m. and flew with the rising sun, which looked brilliantly huge in its early morning fireiness. Apart from the sunlight streaming in through the small square windows, I could see very little without craning my neck and then only a few glimpses of Japan before we reached the sea, and later on, snatches of sparse and barren land, which must have been southern Korea. Sometime after this we felt the Dakota begin to turn, in fact, she circled slowly twice before landing at a small airfield. Here we had a 'break' and half-an-hour to stretch our legs, whilst a few more passengers and some stores were loaded on board before taking off again.

What little I did see of Korea from the plane, appeared to be a mixture of barren, craggy hills, with a jigsaw of paddy fields in between them and I suppose that, just as it is in Japan, rice must be the staple diet of these poor people.

We arrived at an airfield at Seoul at 9 a.m. and after disembarking and checking through, I was shown into a tent, where I was given the most welcome cup of scrumptious hot coffee. A few minutes later a jeep from Britcom Z Med. Unit arrived, carrying the Matron, who had kindly come to meet me and soon after this, we were driven to this little hospital which is quite a distance from the airfield.

The hospital is in what was once a Korean school and on arriving I was shown to our quarters, which are quite comfortable even if somewhat primitive in style, each of us having the luxury of a partitioned cubicle, and it is particularly nice to have the privacy of one's own little room to spread out one's belongings.

Today the weather is very much cooler than it was when I arrived last Wednesday, and I've just had to borrow an enormous khaki sweater from one of the Medical Officers, because I have only brought my tropical kit with me - tho' no doubt it will soon be sizzling hot again. But I must try and fill in some more details about 'life' in this small medical unit, which is sometimes rudely referred to as "The Bastard". This is because it is not only very temporary but also of doubtful origin!

Despite the nickname, we seem to be a small Commonwealth unit, having a British C.O., Australian Matron, and a Canadian Adjutant. Until recently there were seven Sisters in all serving in the hospital, but two Canadians have recently left to go under canvas a little further up, so that now there are just two Australians (one of whom is the Matron, who is quite young and very helpful too) and three of us Q.A.s - Jess Milton the senior - a Captain, Irene Chesters, another Lieutenant, a little bit older than I am, and of course me!

Our meals are taken in the 'mixed' mess, by this I mean that everyone, Medical Officers - Sisters - Admin. Officers etc., plus anybody else who just happens to be passing through, all feed together, at one long table in the 'dining-room' and this is quite a pleasant change for us (to escape from the all-female confines of a Sisters Mess!) The food so far seems to be quite delicious - we even had steak with sweetcorn last night, and real strawberry icecream - the latter had been flown over from the U.S.A. So you can guess that we are living on American rations - absolutely gorgeous too, except I am sure that I shall put on pounds through guzzling too much. The others have warned me that I shall get tired of such luxuries - apparently we have turkey regularly once a week.

As I said, our little hospital unit is located in what I think must have once been a school, with its own collection of rather shabby and battered buildings; those have since been converted into the hospital, messes and various living quarters necessary for the members of Britcom Z and all these buildings are conveniently enclosed in their own small compound. We have roughly three 'wards' (in the classrooms) and we have noticed that when our patients are first admitted, they all seem to be utterly astounded to discover that not only are their beds made up with crisply laundered sheets but that there are also 'real Sisters' here to nurse them!

On duty we just wear our grey uniform dresses (no scarlet capes because it is the hot season) but without our traditional veils. Although we can manage to get the patients' sheets reasonably well laundered, it's impossible for the laundry to cope with veil starching, so that it makes a nice change to be 'capless' for once.

The little glimpse I have had of the Koreans so far, has given me the impression that they are a very different race from the Japanese, appearing to be much more of a peasant stock. I also remember that they were occupied by the Japanese until fairly

Britcom Z nurses in Seoul, 2 June 1953 (Coronation Day). Miss Gillian Hall is on the right.

G. McNair

The front entrance of Britcom Z Medical Unit, Seoul.

recently, and since then for almost the last three years they have been fighting for survival in this horribly cruel war, so it's little wonder that the few I have seen all looked so incredibly glum.

Looking across from the Unit, we can see in the distance that there are a great number of tiny huts and awful shack-like dwellings together and stretching on upwards to the slopes of the barren hills opposite. As far as I can gather, most of the civilian population seems to live in absolute squalor. However, I think there must be some type of school nearby, because at regular times during the day, we can hear the chattering of young voices.

Help! It's almost 4.15 p.m. and I had better dash to take my turn in the shower, or I shall miss it. Next time I write, I must tell you about our rather ingenious sanitary arrangements, but in the meantime I'd better grab my sponge bag and towels, not forgetting my cute little blue Korean bath-shoes (Matron had kindly provided each of us with a pair to wear in the shower block), they are made from rubber, in a Turkish style with upturned pointed toes, and apparently are much favoured by the local Korean ladies.

Wednesday 3rd June.

If only you could see the utter desolation of everything surrounding us, the squalor and the filthy hovels (sometimes these look no bigger than rabbit hutches, with almost the same foetid smells) that these impoverished people exist in. The poor little children with their grubby faces, runny noses, and tattered patched clothing, are pushed out on the streets by their elders to sell Korean cakes, cigarettes and chewing gum. 'You buy chewing gum lady?' No doubt both having been pinched from the U.S. Army stores!

Apparently many hundreds of Korean children have been orphaned as result of this beastly war. Fortunately, most of them are now living in orphanages, many of which are organised by the Armed Forces out here. Our Unit helps to support one and I would very much like to visit it one day if I can. But at the moment, Major Black, our Q.M. (who is one of its chief organisers) doesn't want me to go, because he says that 'it is too sad to see'.

Britcom Z, as I think I've already mentioned, is only a temporary hospital in what must have originally been quite a modern school - built in the 1930's style with a long flat roof with three floors on one side of a central staircase and with two floors on the other. All the windows, and there are many of them, particularly as they are from floor to ceiling along the staircase, seem to be small panes of glass, similar to our Crittal windows at home - only some of the panes are missing.

Our living quarters which are close to the hospital, are situated in a smaller four-storied building of a much older design. In the front of this there are about half-a-dozen wide stone steps leading up to what must have been two front doors and I suppose that these could have been the separate entrances for boys and girls to the original school house.

Despite the modern appearance of our hospital, there is no running water available, so that every drop that is needed has to be carried up in cans, which at times can be a little inconvenient. On the other hand, it is really amazing how quickly one adapts to a tapless situation and consequently manages very well.

We are a medical, not a surgical unit because of the lack of water for surgery. So our sick lads are really only short-stay patients. Being a temporary hospital, we make a

G. McNair
Korean demonstrators against the armistice passing Britcom Z, 11 June 1953.

I. T. Stratford
Entertainment for the children in a back street in Seoul, September 1952.

very good 'stop-gap' between the Field Hospitals (e.g. the Norwegian MASH has an outstanding reputation for coping with all sorts of surgical emergencies), and the Britcom General in Kure, which as you know is our huge base hospital in Japan. The 'boys' who are admitted here are always so pleased to see us and they seem to be a wonderful mixture of Commonwealth troops. We do have a large turnover, with most of them returning to the front both rested and recovered, which I suppose is the real purpose of our being here.

In the morning, we Sisters are called by our little Korean girl, who brings us each a jug of hot water, so that it's very easy to have a quick 'bird bath' in one's cubby-hole. As you know, we can shower each evening if there's time. The shower block which is in constant use by one section of the Unit or another, is located in what were either old stables or a barn, and the Army have rigged up an ingenious device consisting of 5 or 6 old 5 gallon petrol cans, which seem to magically fill with warm water, so that when one gently tugs the string, the can tilts forward and the water sprinkles down, giving sufficient time to soap and rinse quickly before it has finished! We all shower together, no privacy, but again it's amazing how quickly one becomes accustomed to this and even to the four seater ladies only 'Thunderbox'! So far the only time I have felt any embarrassment in this respect, was when I recently found myself sitting on the wooden seat next to Matron. Nice as she really is it did rather put me off!

The floor of the shower house is covered in rather crumbly and broken red bricks and this is the reason for wearing our rubber Korean shoes. We also have to put up with quite an audience when it is Sisters' shower-time because most of the up-patients seem to automatically congregate at the hospital windows to watch and whistle their encouragement as we troop across clutching our towels, shoes and spongebags. However, it was a wise Matron who remarked sometime ago - 'It is when they stop whistling at you, that you need to worry!'

Just occasionally one hears the distant gunfire and last night I heard some bombs a good way off, and we were told today that there was a pretty fierce battle a few nights ago at the Hook in which about twenty of our British boys were killed. You see there really is a war going on out here and it seems a pity that people at home do not take much interest in what's going on.

The Coronation has meant a very great deal to us although we are far from home. Yesterday, 2nd June, was quite a busy day for us, starting with all the patients and staff drinking a Loyal Toast to Her Majesty at 12 noon. We did hardly any work. Later on I went with another Q.A. to the City Stadium (which is not far from us) to watch the Sports Events which were being held there as part of the 1st Commonwealth Division's celebrations. There are also tennis courts (so that my tennis racquet might just be useful after all!) as well as two magnificent swimming pools, but so far I've not discovered these.

We had turkey for dinner plus all the trimmings, and after this, we change into the few glad rags that we have with us, only uniform of course, but this time dressed in our grey dresses, and red capes - (I had to borrow one of Jess' because officially we are in tropical dress and mine are in Kure) - cuffs, and we wore our veils too, to look as smart as we possibly could, because we had all been invited to a special Coronation Cocktail party.

Everybody was there. I have never seen so many Colonels! I was introduced to the Commander-in-Chief, Maxwell D. Taylor, a 3 Star Yankee General, who looked very young and he addressed me as Ma'am! Champagne was running like water at this party and we had all sorts of nice eats to mop it up with. Whilst I was there, someone told me that today the Gunners had been firing red, white and blue smoke at the Gooks (our nickname for the North Korean Commies). I'm not sure how true this is but it wouldn't surprise me!

The Anglican Cathedral was absolutely packed with people attending Divine Service last Sunday (31st May) and as far as I could see almost every member of the sixteen United Nations countries serving in Korea, were represented. To our great surprise, Irene and I discovered that together with a nice lady missionary doctor sitting nearby, we three were the only women present in this huge congregation. This service was impressive: the lesson was read by Lt. Col. H. C. L. Dimsdale M.C., Welsh Guards, and at the conclusion when we all stood stiffly to attention to sing the National Anthem, the effect was overwhelming.

As I've previously mentioned, Anne my friend from Kure, was posted to Britcom Z soon after I was and she had been so helpful, most especially about taking me out and about with her when I am off duty. You see, because we are rather vulnerable, none of us is allowed to leave the hospital compound, unless we go out in pairs. We also have to tell Matron exactly where we are going and at what time we expect to return, and because there are so few of us, it happens quite frequently that one can be the only Sister off duty in the Mess....

Anyway, Anne is blessed with having her own jeep, plus driver to guard her, to use when she needs to visit British servicemen who are being nursed in other hospitals in and around Seoul. Yesterday she took me with her so that I could visit some of the British soldiers in the American Hospital, which is not so far from here. In comparison to Britcom Z, this seemed to be a colossal place, although in appearance it was just as drab and bare as our own little unit.

The Americans are doing a magnificent job there and luckily have good facilities for most types of surgery. Everybody I met was so kind and friendly to me and I really admire all that they are managing to do.

Tuesday, 9 June.

Living here is such an interesting experience and one is never quite certain of what is going to happen next! At the moment the Peace Treaty talks sound as though they might well be fruitful, although the South Koreans themselves don't seem to be very keen about this and appear to be upset. In fact, during the last few days there have been fairly large demonstrations in the city and even from the hospital we can see long pathetic-looking processions of people demonstrating against the Treaty.

These are made up mainly of elderly men and women, some of whom are very old, and children, lots and lots of children, some shouting and some carrying banners with UNIFICATION OR DEATH painted in large letters across them. Most of the adults are dressed in typical peasant fashion quaint broad straw hats and baggy trousers for men - long skirts and Turkish shaped shoes for the women. It's so sad to see them shambling in this weary, thin, long line and I just cannot understand why they don't want peace instead of this cruel war which they are still experiencing.

At the moment, because of the rather tense situation amongst the civilian population, we are all 'Confined to Barracks' and well protected by our six armed guards at the hospital gates. Life is full of suprises too, because we even had a slight air raid last night. Needless to say we had all gone to bed early only to be woken rather abruptly by a couple of big bangs! We quickly leapt out of our beds, threw on our slacks and jerseys and ran over to the hospital to evacuate the patients if necessary. However, all was quiet on arrival and after waiting for some time, we were instructed to return to the Mess and thankfully back to bed. As far as we know, the Gooks (rude name for the N. Koreans) only dropped a couple of small bombs.

From the small glimpse that I've so far managed to see of this part of Korea, there does appear to be far more greenery than there is in Japan. Indeed, in some areas which are well out of the city, the scenery is very pretty. The earth is actually a shade of deep red, not unlike that of south Devon, the rich lush grass combining with the bright foliage of the trees to give an unusually brilliant shade of green. But I really think that to see wide stretches and flat fields of grass again has impressed me more than anything, after living for many months with the sparsely terraced slopes of Japan, much as I admire them.

The Korean national costumes are quite different from the Japanese. The ladies wear short bolero jackets which are usually white and sometimes have a black braided edging. Under this is a long dress with an Empire style waistline with a full skirt and of course, the little pair of light blue (often made from rubber) Turkish style shoes peeping out from beneath it. The plain, but graceful effect, is enhanced by their beautiful straight, jet black hair, which is usually drawn back from their faces and is either worn twisted into a bun or as long thick plait, if young. The elderly men are usually dressed in a loose white robe, and a pair of baggy trousers, quite often topped by a battered straw hat and similar shoes to the women's. On the whole they appear to be very much a peasant race, with the women still doing their washing in the river. In fact, the day I arrived here, I actually saw them beating the clothes Italian style, in the famous river Han.

From what I can gather, I believe that there have been recent reports in the English newspapers about the air raids that we have been having in Seoul. Originally I had hoped that this news would not have reached your papers, mainly because I was afraid that you might worry about it. However, now that it has, please do not worry, because these little excitements are nothing compared to those of the last war and quite honestly we all treat them as a big joke. In fact, we wait up for 'Bed-check Charlie' every night before bothering to go to bed, because, conveniently enough, he and his companions always seem to turn up at the same rather early hour! Personally, I think that the Gooks are trying out some mild form of psychological warfare, because the raids really are only what one could describe as 'nuisance raids'. But having said that, I must admit that yesterday they changed their silly old tactics and we had no less than six warnings in twenty-four hours. Tonight we have already had two, but no noise at all. Actually last night they did drop a couple of bombs, but luckily for us, they fell a good distance away from here. In any case, we've heard on the grapevine that the Gooks haven't much in the way of explosives and that they are just using up secondhand stuff left over from World War II! I don't suppose that many of those can 'go off' if you know what I mean, so please don't worry because we are all perfectly safe here.

Personally too, I am extremely lucky to be on night duty whilst all this is going on, because at least I am able to sleep during the day, while the other poor Sisters have to get up and stay on duty until the All Clear is sounded. You see when the siren goes, the Day Sisters shoot over to the hospital, ready to evacuate the stretcher patients from the first floor to the ground floor corridors during a proper raid. We don't have any shelters, or tin hats unlike some of the other Units around, but on the other hand, we are a hospital and we should be O.K.

The South Koreans still appear to be very upset about accepting the Peace Treaty and there have been a considerable number of demonstrations against it in different parts of the city. Yesterday I managed to 'escape' from the hospital compound for a brief and welcome spell (only the second in ten days). Matron, another Sister and I travelled by jeep to buy some of the necessities of life at the P.X. in Seoul - that is the U.S. Forces equivalent to our NAAFI. During our return journey we met a large demonstration comprised mainly of neatly dressed schoolgirls, wearing their attractive navy-blue sailor suits style uniform. Many of them were carrying banners, placards and chanting; the chanting was almost continuous. Quite honestly I couldn't help some feeling of revulsion at seeing these poor children being caught up in this political mess, and it is always the children who seem to suffer so much.

For example, whilst we were driving through the city, we stopped for five minutes to buy some flowers at a little florists (this was really a very small flower shop, not a florists in the true sense). Flowers are an expensive luxury in Seoul and most of the ones on display looked decidedly scraggy too. On returning to our jeep we found it and our driver completely surrounded by a band of tattered, ragged little beggar boys, shouting and demanding money. Irene and I hopped into the back of the jeep, with Matron gracefully climbing into the front seat beside the driver and just as we were driving off, both Irene and I noticed one poor little wretch plunge his small thin hand into the side pocket of Matron's skirt to pinch her fountain pen. I suppose had he been successful, he most probably would have tried to flog it back to us next time we went out - 'You buy Parker pen lady?' But isn't it desperately tragic to witness this sort of thing in 1953? What future hope do these poor kids have?

Friday, 19 June.

'Bedcheck Charlie' eventually paid us a visit last night, but this time he turned up much later at about 3.30 a.m. For some time previously we had had a number of first warnings (over the radio) before he finally emerged. As Night Sister and responsible for the hospital, I receive the first warning alerts (this is the stage prior to full alert and the sounding of the siren), but immediately after this warning, the whole of the Unit is automatically 'blacked out' so that I seem to spend most of my time stumbling in complete darkness, until I've managed to light the few emergency candles that we are allowed to use!

Because of the lateness of the raid last night, my office soon turned into a running buffet for all and sundry, including the upstairs patients who had to be evacuated to the ground floor corridor, and the poor, tired day staff who were on their feet once again. All needed lots of tea, and because the teapots were far too small to merit the number of cups required, I decided to show the orderlies how to make tea in a bucket (a clean shiny one!).At the same time, I remembered with gratitude, previous instructions once given to me as a very new Sister when a similar crisis occurred on my ward in Aldershot. This was by my then Duputy Matron, Major Agnes McGeary, QARANC of Chindit fame, and from whose great experience I soon learned how to cope under awkward circumstances. Anyway, it was quite a long vigil and our buckets of hot, strong, sweet tea were much appreciated, as we ladled out 'seconds' into the waiting mugs. Patients and staff were cracking jokes about how the Gooks have only some old-fashioned equipment left and how if they do manage to drop any bombs, they do this by throwing them over the sides of the planes! Last but not least, my office and tea-making area has now been nicknamed 'Jill's Grill'!

Now I must check that my patients are alright; they are such lovely boys, with a terrific sense of humour too. My only regret is that they are in hospital for only a short time that we don't have chance to really get to know them. The majority of them sleep like logs, right through any or our minor type air raids, presumably because they are so accustomed to heavy gunfire etc., that these tiny little bangs mean nothing to them.

Wednesday, 29 July.

Just a hasty and last Forces Letter to you from the Land of the Morning Calm - to say how truly delighted we all were to hear that the Armistice was signed on Monday 27th July - it really is such wonderful news.

To be honest, I think that most people have taken the news rather quietly, although we were all invited to an impromptu celebration that evening at the Officers' Club in Seoul, and Jess and I and some of the Medical Officers went. There were lots of people there, and everybody seemed unbelievably pleased about the cease fire, tho' several I met were hoping that it wouldn't be breached. We had some champagne to drink and one or two of the younger and more high-spirited members, actually jumped not only in delight, but *into* the small swimming pool- fully clothed, and still holding their glasses high!

Chapter 14

NURSING ABOARD H.M. HOSPITAL SHIP *MAINE*

By Ruth Stone, Matron (Retired) Q.A.R.N.N.S.

"One of Britain's most useful contributions to the United Nations' effort in the Korean War has been Her Majesty's Hospital Ship *Maine*." These were the words of Lord Fraser of North Cape, First Sea Lord, in 1950. How could we remotely have foreseen, on joining this floating hospital in 1949 in Malta, the ultimate role of the ageing twenty-six year old vessel which was to be our home and workplace for the next adventurous two years.

The specific reason behind the commissioning was the serious turn of events during the Chinese Civil War in 1949, which found H.M.S. *Amethyst* trapped in the Yangtze River. If the situation deteriorated, the evacuation of the 150 or so patients, normally at the R.N. Hospital, Hong Kong, would be imperative.

So, with a peace-time complement, the Medical Division, consisting of a Principal Medical Officer, 4 Medical Officers, 1 Dental Officer, a Matron and 4 Nursing Sisters of Queen Alexandra's Royal Naval Nursing Service, 6 Naval V.A.D.s (the first to serve afloat), 1 Wardmaster and 30 Sick Berth Staff; *Maine* was dispatched to Far Eastern waters under the experienced and versatile seamanship of the Commodore Royal Fleet Auxiliary and his nucleus of seasoned senior officers - not forgetting the one hundred home sick Maltese deckhands and Thomas the dignified black and white ship's cat.

From the start, the ship was a continual challenge to the professional resources and ingenuity of the Master. In 1940, under the name of *Leonardo Da Vinci*, she was subsequently salved and patched up by the British and expensively refitted as a hospital ship and placed in reserve. One would have thought that now not a bolt in this pristine ship could go adrift. Alas, this was not so. With such a history she was much weakened structually. Seams began to open in the furnaces, air conditioning blew feebly and steering gear failed.

In March 1950 we accompanied the Far Eastern Fleet on routine manoeuvres in the Philippines. A large detachment of R.N. and U.S.N. ships gathered there to participate in a joint communications exercise. Our work as a Base Hospital Ship was interesting. We then sailed back to Hong Kong and after a short spell there we joined the Fleet on their Summer Cruise to Japan. Daily we marvelled that the ship had not been recalled to the U.K. and from time to time considered ourselves forgotten by our masters at the Admiralty.

Then, at Kobe on 25 June 1950, sudden news came of the North Korean invasion of South Korea. All Royal Navy ships were placed at the disposal of the U.S. Naval Command.

On 8 July, *Maine* sailed for Sasebo to be ready to receive casualties and take them back to Japan. We spent the day preparing the 300 cots, storing drug cupboards and assembling equipment for the unknown onslaught to come. We had at that time only two Sick Berth Attendants on each ward and a goodly percentage of these were Z Reservists. One remarkable Leading Hand improved and devised, most efficiently, under-water-seal drainage apparatus from sterile intravenous sets: quite a departure from his civilian occupation as a lumberjack. For several weeks, *Maine* was the only hospital ship on the scene of operations. Between 16 July and 16 August 1950, we made eight trips between Pusan and Japan, evacuating a total of 1,849 casualties, nearly all of them American soldiers. On 29 August, we were at Pusan when H.M.S. *Ceylon* and H.M.S. *Unicorn* (a light carrier) arrived bringing the 1st Battalion Argyll and Sutherland Highlanders and the 1st Battalion Middlesex Regiment. Sadly, three weeks later, we received several Argylls who had been badly burnt from a wrongly aimed napalm air attack.

I can clearly remember the hectic activity alongside the quays of dusty Pusan harbour, the fleets of field ambulances arrived carrying wounded from the hospital trains. At the bottom of our gangway, the Senior Medical Officer and Wardmaster assessed the gravity of the general condition of each man and the appropriate Ward was allocated accordingly.

The dangerously and seriously ill were directed to the one and only ward with air conditioning: less critically injured to those wards adjacent and the walking wounded to the water-line wards a deck below. Simultaneously, two surgeons would operate on as many urgent cases as they could, occasionally ashore in field hospital tents whilst loading was underway. These are often amputations, since gangrene was the great enemy and of course it was not always possible to operate in really rough weather at sea especially as in early autumn the typhoon season presented a further hazard.

Medically speaking, a typhoon restricted the work of operations and from the point of view of seamanship, it could add another five days to the normal transit time in order to steer safely through the storm.

With immediate treatment and medication instructions written on luggage labels attached to the casualties' wrists, together with scanty previous notes scrawled by doctors in the forward casualty clearing stations, South Korean soldiers carried the stretchers to the wards and the loading of these weary and bedraggled wounded was generally achieved in twelve hours. The sailing time back to Japan through the Shimonoseki Straits and into the inland sea normally took two to three days. It was impossible to reduce this period as the allies had not yet declared the Japanese swept channels free of mines.

This part of the journey was the most strenuous time for the medical division, complemented and equipped as we were for peace-time duties. The two Day Sisters and Nurses rarely found their work done before midnight and the sole Night Sister made her weary way to her bunk about mid-day. The Theatre Sister was on duty or on call continuously. The 6 V.A.D.s staffed the Officers' Ward and were invaluable with their excellent nursing and tireless attention to detail. It should be mentioned, also, that the versatile Deck Berth Staff were magnificent during the crisis and stood killing watches at the height of the conflict from 0800-1200 hours, followed by 5 hours off, then from 0700-2100 hours, with an additional skeleton night staff.

Our Matron, Miss Barbara Nockolds, relieved in the operating theatre, ran the Officers' Ward and also a small below water-line Ward where the badly shell-shocked patients were housed. In fact she was everywhere, working well into the night like everyone else. Ralph Izzard, who was the Special War Correspondent for "The Daily Mail" and who often sailed with us, wrote of her in the edition of 17 September 1950, "A rare, inspiring, imperturbable and supremely capable woman

The British hospital ship *Maine* at Kure, Japan.

who never seemed to tire". Anyone who had anything to do with her thought the same and, not surprisingly she was much respected and loved.

Randolph Churchill was "The Daily Telegraph" War Correspondent and he also sailed in *Maine* from time to time, writing a blistering report on the conditions and inadequacy of the resources of *Maine* during this war period, into which the ship had been unwittingly tossed. The water-line Wards required that the portholes be secured when at sea and as the temperatures there registered 90° - 116°F, since these Wards were actually situated over the main generators and furthermore did not have either air conditioning or washing facilities, you can imagine the resemblance to Dante's Inferno as we descended the ramp to cope with some 80 - 100 battle soiled and dehydrated walking wounded. But, in spite of the lack of normal, basic nursing conditions, the wounded were so grateful just to be able to lie down in comparative safety and sleep. Numerous large jugs of water and lime-juice were placed in strategic positions and all these battle fatigued patients were sedated to spite the noise of the all too near ship's engines below.

At the other end of the ship, and a deck above, the critically injured were amassed; the dying in free-swinging cots to lessen the effects of the ship's pitching. It was generally accepted that all those with penetrating abdominal wounds should have colostomies; all chest wounds should be treated with some form of under-water-seal drainage, and head injuries, especially of the neck region, should undergo a tracheotomy operation. On admission to the ward, and sometimes at the gangway, every plaster was bi-valved and every soldier with a wound or burn had an intra-muscular injection of penicillin, a.m. and p.m. In those days this life-saving drug was prepared in a suspension of beeswax: quite diabolical to draw up speedily into a syringe but here our Dental Officer and his assistant came to the rescue. They toiled from bed to bed from one end of the ship to the other and each evening they began all over again. This they somehow achieved in addition to attending to intricate jaw and facial reconstructions which presented themselves on each trip.

As far as the Nursing Sisters were concerned, the dressing seemed endless and the added nightmare of discovering maggots in the wounds, inside plasters and under

Taking wounded aboard while at sea from tank landing craft.

scalps (and even first colostomy dressings produced thousands of these horrors), made our work doubly traumatic! But, with just rest, fluids and food, the majority of the patients showed a remarkable improvement after their short stay with us when they were transferred to their next medical care haven either in America or in Commonwealth Base Hospitals in Kure or Osaka.

Sadly, we did not carry a Chaplain of our own, but occasionally one sailed with us in order to join a destroyer or frigate flotilla. They were truly God-sent as many men died without the comfort of the last rites of their church or a final blessing. It was indeed an added concern to us that this was so.

Americans do not bury their dead at sea or on foreign soil, but return the corpses to their homeland. Those that died aboard had to be laid aft, and because of the heat, precious ice had to be placed over them at two hourly intervals. The overworked dispensary Leading Hand had this unsavoury task to perform, but was helped on occasions by the war reporters to whom we were 'giving a lift'. Sometimes at Pusan the hospital trains disgorged not patients but hundreds of white painted coffins which were then loaded on store ships returning to the U.S.A. The organisation for receiving patients in Osaka was highly efficient and they were disembarked speedily to a fleet of waiting ambulances and medical coaches. The dead went off first, covered with the flag of their country, whilst appropriate music was played by a military band assembled on the quayside. A sad moment for all but the last tribute was carried out with reverence.

R. Stone

Q.A.R.N.N.S. nurses on *Maine.* Misses Nockolds, Walshaw, Hesmondhagh, Stone, Hereford.

M. Wood née Hereford

Disembarking wounded at Osaka, Japan.

F. W. A. Nutt

Britcom General Hospital, Kure, Japan.

Immediately after this event and when all patients were ashore, more feverish activity of a different nature continued in the wards. Beds were stripped and disinfected and when the fresh linen was delivered on board (since our Ship's laundry could only cope with uniforms) the beds were made up in preparation for the next convoy. A bag containing toilet necessities, playing cards, writing paper, magazines, packets of cigarettes and sweets, supplied by the American Red Cross, was placed inside each locker. Only after completing this task could the medical staff sleep - and often it was for 24 hours.

At times when the *Maine* needed repairs, the British Commonwealth Hospital in Kure, staffed by British and Australian Military Q.A.s, also provided us scope for really hard and interesting work, it being one of the receiving Base Hospitals for the United Nations' wounded. The Naval Sisters worked in pairs in a supernumerary capacity on the 60 bedded wards. The highly qualified and experienced Ward Staff (we were allocated 10 Sisters and 2 Orderlies on the wards) toiled for long hours to ease the pain and distress of the wounded in their care.

Japanese flower-girls came to the wards each morning pushing trollies laden with fresh flowers and foliage of every description. A single arrangement was assembled of simple but breathtaking design and then elevated by a copper pulley to rest a few feet higher than the ward's central light in order that all could see it. At night a little blue spot-light illuminated the masterpiece to the joy and comfort of everyone.

At last, two additional Nursing Sisters arrived together with more Sick Berth Staff. The port became busier and to our relief (in both senses) the advent of the U.S. Hospital Ships *Repose, Haven,* and *Consolation* greatly cheered us. These superbly equipped and purpose built ships, of similar patient capacity, boasted 20 Medical Officers, 41 Sisters and 130 Sick Bay Staff. Compared with our 6 Medical Officers, 6 Sisters and about 50 Sick Berth Staff, it was undoubtedly bliss. So *Maine* was able to leave this war zone and take some badly wounded and seriously burnt soldiers from the Argyll and Sutherland Highlanders and the Gloucestershire Regiments to Hong Kong.

And so it went on: repeated trips interlaced with luxurious interludes of picnic parties and tours organised by kind British civilians ashore, not to mention all the entertainment we received from the ships in company. We were exceedingly spoilt, I fear, but the common danger we shared forged a strong esprit de corps and lasting friendships which even today are remembered, not least among the South Koreans themselves whose Government is very generous in its thanks and hospitality to all those who fought and survived. I and others experienced this on a delightful revisit in 1981.

The services of *Maine* were recognised in 1950 by a special message of appreciation and thanks from Admiral Joy, U.S.N. Finally, a Republic of Korea Presidential Citation dated 20 April 1952 was awarded. A translation was published a year later in a Special Routine General Order by Lieutenant General H. Wells, C.B.E., D.S.O., Commander-in-Chief, British Commonwealth Forces, Korea.

Memory can play tricks after some thirty years, but most of my two years service spent in *Maine* remains crystal clear and events are recalled in detail. I shall always be thankful for the unique experience this episode afforded.

Chapter 15

WEST COAST OPERATIONS

By Peter Shore

I joined H.M.S. *Opossum* as an Able Seaman at the age of eighteen, when she was recommissioned in April 1952, after years of idleness at Chatham. H.M.S. *Opossum* was a frigate of 1,375 tons displacement. Her armament was three twin 4 inch gun mountings, 2 pdr Pom-Poms, Oerlikon A.A. guns and anti-submarine missiles and depth charges. Her Commander was J.C. Cartwright, D.S.C. H.M.S. *Crane* was a sister ship. In January 1953, I experienced my first patrol off the enemy coast. The following are my diary entries, without change of any kind. Del (Delphine) was a girlfriend.

Friday 9 January 1953

Middle Watch today - lifebuoy sentry. Weather was unusually mild and though there was rather a heavy swell, I felt quite comfortable. As we changed into Cruising Watches; Red Watch has the forenoon Watch, which passed peaceably enough.

Feeling O.K. today, and borrowed back my book - "Kon Tiki Expedition" - and turned in at 13.30 to read. Fell asleep about 14.30 and didn't get up until nearly 18.00!! We have the First tonight so I can see us missing pictures again, hope we get a chance tomorrow night.

"Jimmy" (First Lieutenant) spoke to us over the Ammunition Broadcast, saying we would anchor in the Han River Estuary tonight and proceeding up river in the Forenoon on a high tide!!!

Should be fun and games? Writing to Del tonight before going on watch.

Saturday 10 January

Well we've arrived, and as to yet it is pretty safe and we are now anchored in a large bay about 6 miles from the mouth of the river. This afternoon Sub. Lt. Mackenzie, Mick Muscett and Browney went off in a borrowed junk to survey the Bay - surroundings and bearings etc.

Earlier this afternoon we took an American Officer on board, who, it seems, will be directing the bombardment in the morning. We are indirectly sheltered by friendly islands, and tomorrow we are trying to bombard a village by firing blindly over the top, spotting is being done by "Subby" - God knows where the shells will eventually land? Came off watch tonight at 20.00. There is a film on but I don't feel interested - guess I'll finish this and then a letter and turn in - tired as usual.

Sunday 11 January

Pipe down this morning at 10.00. Captain said prayers, and gave us general news of past and future events.

Peter Shore on H.M.S. *Opossum.*

H.M.S. *Opossum* firing 4 inch guns.

Ice and snow seen whilst on watch this morning, drifting past with the current, though according to the thermometer, the temperature was only 31°F - not really so cold as all that.

Bombarding this afternoon an enemy island about 7 miles distant - hope it doesn't last too long for we've the "first dog" as well (Middle Watch) tonight - so there hadn't better be films on our messdeck. Fired 8 rounds on "B" gun this afternoon - won't know the results until later. "Just Red Watch's luck".

Firing again at 18.00 tonight. Decided at the last minute to give 6 fast salvos before we go off watch - and then we only fired 4. God knows what we were shooting at, only hope it was worth the effort. Middle Watch tonight.

Monday 12 January

"Hell Fire Corner"!! Talk about cold, the temperature is now 10°F - 12°F below freezing and is still dropping steadily. It is sheer suicide to take our gloves off - as for our toes - they are things of the past. In many places on the Upper Deck, water was frozen solid to an inch thickness and is treacherous to walk on the deck fast.

The messdecks are now being heated by steam heated air through the messdeck fans. It is nice and warm admittedly but not at 19.00. It is getting a bit too much.

Turned in this afternoon until 15.00. Have the First tonight, and as we intend to reach the oiler *Wave Chief* either tonight or tomorrow morning, we are wondering whether we shall go alongside in the dark tonight - I sincerely pray we don't for it will be sheer madness on this icy deck.

Alongside the oiler tonight - the ice on the upper deck is the best part of two inches thick - the whole fo'c'sle is covered - and believe it or not - the Old Man decides to come alongside. When we came in the light of the oiler we could see that the bows and all of "A" Gun was covered in a thick film of ice. Was it freezing coming alongside! Reward was one bag of mail, so our labours were not in vain.

Had a letter from Mum - read at 01.00??

Tuesday 13 January

Arrived at our Patrol Area this morning about 10.00 and took up station on the landward side of the *Crane* who had arrived the day before. This evening we received the call that an American seaplane was forced down and couldn't take off again. We answered the call, and tried to come alongside but the sea was too rough - we then launched one whaler, but was useless - in doing so we had three cases of frostbite and exposure in the whaler's crew. The whaler was then lost - carried away in the swell later.

A line was eventually passed to the plane after some heart-thumping accidents and near misses, and she was secured astern about 100ft. At 22.00, Lower Deck was cleared, and an attempt was made to haul her up to the ship's side - oil had been put down to smooth its passage. By now a tug was standing by. After about 30 mins solid sweating on the grass line, we had the plane within touching distance and the grass suddenly parted, the plane immediately floated astern owing to the swell. It was much too late to get another line across, so now it is up to the tug to work on her. Hands dismissed very fed up that after getting her so far we lost her. Covered in oil and filth - what a night! I wonder what tomorrow brings?

Wednesday 14 January

A very cold Middle. Was heaven to turn in. Today was spent at anchor just about 10,000 yds. from the shore in our Patrol Sector. A tug and a Landing Craft (Rocket) kept us company. Pictures on board in the aft messdeck tonight. "The Snipe" not a bad film - makes a change.

Thursday 15 January

Received mail from *Crane* this morning, but of course none for me.

I really expected one but maybe it will be my turn next. Typical *Opossum* move - we took mail off the boat sent by *Crane* but forgot to give her our mail to go down to the oiler, so we passed the morning away by passing a heaving line over with the mail secured into it.

We all held our breath as it swung between two ships - quite a chuck up when it reached safely. Detailed off this afternoon to act as "coverguard" to a minesweeper who was sweeping close inshore. As we arrived she just started getting shelled, so we came up in range, but couldn't locate the gun emplacement. We called for the help of 3 planes, who on arrival found the position. This turned into attack with bombs and rockets. It only took three attacks before the place on the hillside was covered in smoke. We were lucky in having a front row seat of the attack, which was quite successful.

First Watch tonight, with a splitting headache, I shall be glad when midnight comes around.

Pay Day tomorrow - I hope, I hope, I hope!!!

Friday 16 January

Brrrr! cold isn't the word. This morning we closed up for bombardment in firing about 12 rounds each gun. Results showed that we had 4 salvos in the target area and 3 broadsides as direct hits, which was darned good considering the weather - 22° below.

Ice everywhere at 13.00. Ice floes began to float down on the tide and it wasn't long before we were firmly wedged in ice. It took the engines at half ahead 170 revs to free ourselves.

We then left the ice and crashed our way through until we came into clear water. H.M.C.S. *Athabascan* arrived this evening at 16.30 and anchored about a mile inshore.

Supposed to have mail onboard her for us - but she's keeping it until tomorrow - roll on tomorrow.

Cleared out my album tonight wondering what I shall do with all the "female" photos, return them (cost a fortune in stamps) send 'em to Del? Keep them or burn them, I wonder which?

Ice on the deck of H.M.S. *Opossum*

P. Shore

The 4 inch shells of 'A' Gun, H.M.S. *Opossum*

Chapter 16

ONE DARK NIGHT IN KOREA

By Reuben Holroyd

Ian E. Kaye's poem "Friend or......?" reminds me of what was probably the single most frightening experience I had in Korea. Not from Chinese artillery or mortar fire nor from any activity by the enemy. This is an account of an event which took place five months after the cessation of hostilities in Korea.

When my unit, The Duke of Wellington's Regiment, finished its tour of duty towards the end of October 1953, and the Regiment departed for their next posting at Gibraltar, I along with several hundred National Servicemen, were left behind in Korea to complete our tour of duty. Most were transferred to the North Staffordshire Regiment, who had relieved the "Dukes", with the exception of myself and a few others, who had less service to do, and we were "Posted in lieu of regimental route" to 29 Brigade, Main and Rear Divisional Headquarters Units, for general duties. I was posted to Rear Divisional HQ located at the new Kansas Line location south of Gloster Valley and the village of Sinam-ni, where I came by the cushy number of Post Corporal. By chance, my close friend, Derek Lomas, had also been posted at this time to 29 Brigade HQ, but north of Gloster Valley.

On Saturday, 2nd January 1954, I decided to have a day off (Rear Divisional Headquarters was run along those easy lines!) and visit my old pal Derek. I had no trouble thumbing a lift north through Gloster Valley to 29 Brigade Headquarters, where I spent a pleasant day as an unofficial guest at the officers' mess. I found myself in a situation that guaranteed I would be well fed and watered for Derek had been promoted i/c waiters, I believe, and he certainly appeared to be running the show.

Time passed swiftly in such convivial company and I was surprised when Last Post sounded, which reminded me that it was time to be on my way to Rear Divisional Headquarters, before I was missed. Tendering my farewells, I wandered down the hillside to the camp entrance lit by two drums of burning petrol, where I stood talking to the sentry in the hope of picking up a southbound vehicle.

Chatting to the sentry I soon realised that beyond the immediate area illuminated by the flames of the burning petrol visibility was zero. The moon and stars were obscured by heavy clouds which created a dense fog at ground level, with not a glimmer of light to be seen in any direction. After awhile it became apparent that there would be no transport moving so late on a Saturday night. I was faced with the prospect of making my way back through Gloster Valley in pitch darkness and on foot. It was this worrying thought that kept me warming myself by the fires, hoping for transport to come any minute. Eventually I resigned myself to the fact that there was nothing left for me to do but to start walking.

Envying the sentry standing by his fire, I said farewell to him and set off for Gloster Valley. For the first two or three hundred yards I coped well and made reasonable progress. The road was straight and to some extent lit by the fires in the background. However, as I entered the valley proper and the road became a twisting track, the faint glow of the fires was left behind and it became impossible to see more than a yard ahead.

Unable to see anything clearly, I walked off the track on numerous occasions, stumbling into ditches and tripping over stones and potholes. At one point, where the road diverged for tracked vehicles to ford the stream, another hesitant step took me over a drop of some four feet, landing with a thud on a lower track. Completely disorientated, I decided to remain where I was until visibility improved. Some time later, still laid on my back on the hard frozen ground and looking upwards, I was aware that a breeze had developed and the clouds were moving. Around me the bushes, heavy with frost, swayed and rustled in the icy-cold breeze. I suddenly felt very much alone. I trembled when I remembered the stories of soldiers who had been ambushed by local bandits: the problems arising out of guarding military establishments and camps against determined armed intruders; the sergeant with a knife buried in his chest; of guards caught unawares. (Twice during the following weeks, while acting as guard commander, I was personally attacked, and on one occasion had been knocked unconscious by a blow to the head.) I nervously fingered the revolver which I had bought privately.

The clouds parted slightly and in the pale dim starlight the track became a blurred ribbon of grey which disappeared into an inky blackness. I felt it was time to move. I rose stiffly to my feet, conscious of the freezing temperature of the Korean mid-winter stealing my body-heat. I broke into a jog-trot, trying to keep to the crown of the road, hoping to restore circulation and cover as much distance as possible before the available light vanished again.

About two hundred yards further it did vanish and total darkness returned. By now I had thought of a plan. I would zigzag across the road like a sailing ship in contest with the wind; first one tack then another. Each time I counted the paces until I reached the edge of the road surface, feeling gingerly with my foot for the ground as it fell away or, alternatively, rose into a bank. I felt I made steady if rather hesitant progress towards my destination.

Suddenly I froze; my hair stood on end. What was that I had heard, or had my imagination got out of hand? I listened very carefully without making a move. There was no mistake, the sound that I had heard was of stealthy movement. In the dark and the wilderness to either side of me the stunted growth of shrub moved and rustled. Was it the wind or was I already surrounded by bandits? My imagination worked overtime.

With pounded heart I turned, trying to make as little noise as possible, and retreated twenty paces or so, then dropped to the ground and slid my body off the track and into a two feet deep ditch. As I lay there, I strained my ears for the sounds of movement, but the rising wind blowing through the scrub confused all sound.

Time passed. How long I do not know, but it seemed for ever. Then my senses froze into concentration by the barely audible noise that sounded for all the world like that of a body crab-crawling the ground towards me. I removed the glove from my right hand, drew and cocked the revolver, my mind wincing from the loud click the hammer made, feeling sure that whoever it was out there would have heard it. I stretched my body full length on the ground; the cold embrace of the frozen earth forgotten; holding the pistol in both hands, and wishing I could see my target.

I thought of an old Yorkshire saying that goes: 'The chap who gets his blow in first being thrice blessed', which comforted me as my trigger finger tightened upon the trigger. I debated the merits of firing a warning shot, but decided against such a cautious action as it would surely give away my position and possibly a fusillade in retaliation.

Ages seemed to pass and then, as if on cue, the dark clouds parted and the light of the moon illuminated the scene and a figure crouched in the centre of the road, his head darting from side to side, at the same time pointing a large automatic pistol in all directions. Only one man, so my original fears started to subside; though I eyed the waved pistol, which was still looking for a target, with some trepidation. Suddenly, the pistol cracked and a bullet ricocheted off a rock on the far bank, whining away into the distance. I felt the slightest movement on my part would result in the menacing figure emptying his magazine in my direction, as I attempted to crouch even lower.

After a few moments thought, wondering how best to defuse the situation, I cautiously raised my head and, in the challenge familiar to all soldiers, called: "Halt, who goes there?" It worked wonders! The menacing figure straightened up, lowered the hand that held the pistol, and fired off his number, rank, name and unit. (Vaguely, I recall now that he was a sergeant in the US Marine Corps.) I called out to him to put away his pistol, and this he did, I then climbed out of the ditch and introduced myself; explaining what I was doing in Gloster Valley in the middle of the night.

It was an incredible coincidence: our stories were identical. From visiting friends, and unable to get a lift back to our units, we had stumbled off and on the road; in the process becoming nervous wrecks, until we had encountered each others presence in the fearsome and dark wilderness.

In that awful isolation the two of us conversed, all the energy of nervous tension dissipating through a flurry of questions: "Where do you come from back home?" "How long have you served and how much longer to do in Korea?" "You married? Gotta girl? What's she like?" "You scared?" But even as the words flowed hurriedly, we were both conscious of the need to get on with it and take advantage of the light which the clouds now permitted. Reluctantly, we shook hands and said we hoped we would meet each other again, then we went our separate ways - the American to the north and myself to the south.

With a lighter heart I made steady progress, moving only when the moon stopped playing at hide and seek with the clouds. After half a mile or so I heard the grinding noise of the gears of a heavy vehicle moving at a laboured speed towards me. Out of the darkness the bright headlights dazzled me as I waved for the driver to stop. It was a Scammel recovery truck belonging to the R.E.M.E. detachment at Rear Divisional Headquarters. A couple of familiar faces looked down at me and expressing no surprise at my presence, the driver asked if I had seen a broken down truck further north. "No" I said. "Probably a hoax", he replied, "We're always being sent out on wild goose chases, I'm going back to camp and a warm bed". "Good idea", I said, and thankfully squashed into the cab. In thick fog the Scammel crawled with laboured engine back to camp, to end a most frightening experience.

Wireless set No. 31 back packed on light weight metal 'A' frame.

Pencil and message form.

Tin of 50 free issue cigarettes

Note pad.

Spade.

Cap.

303 Rifle.

Hand held microphone.

Pack covered by shirt contained C7 rations, mess tins, washing gear, sweater and poncho.

Camera case.

Ammunition pouches with belt, bayonet and water bottle.

Field glasses.

Map of target area.

Private Reuben Holroyd of the Signal Platoon, The Duke of Wellington's Regiment, 1953.

H.M.S. *Belfast,* Hong Kong, 1951.

Captain Sir Aubrey St. Clair Ford DSO on the telegraphists' mess deck of H.M.S. *Belfast*, Christmas 1951.

H.M.S. *Belfast* ice-bound near Chodo-Sokto islands off the enemy west coast, 1950

Six inch guns of H.M.S. *Belfast* bombarding coastal batteries on the west coast, 1951.

Studio Medico, H.M.S. Belfast
North Korean and Chinese prisoners captured by Royal Marines and held aboard H.M.S. *Belfast.*

G. David
H.M.N.Z.S. *Taupo* at anchor (left) with H.M.S. *Comus* and H.M.C.S. *Cayuga* oiling from a tanker. Taechong-do anchorage off the enemy west coast, May 1952.

G. David

The Royal Navy helped to keep control of islands off the enemy west coast. Paegnyong-do, August 1952.

G. David

Yongmae-do from a R.O.K. armed junk, August 1952.

G. David
H.M.A.S. *Bataan* going alongside H.M.S. *Ocean* to transfer mail, June 1952.

H.M.S. *Charity,* Taechong-do, February 1952. Taken by Geoffrey David, a R.N. officer serving on H.M.A.S. *Bataan.*

R. Neep

H.M.S. *Charity*, destroyer.

G. David

Transferring Sub. Lieut. Clapp R.N. to an oiler from H.M.A.S. *Bataan*, June 1952.

H.M.S. *Birmingham*, cruiser.

R. Neep

Possibly H.M.S. *Cossack* (D8) and probably H.M.S. *Ocean* oiling from a tanker.

P. Cook

Sea Fury of 801 Squadron landing on H.M.S. *Glory*.

P. Cook

Sea Fury in the crash barrier on H.M.S. *Glory*.

P. Cook
Lt. Mitchell R.N., the pilot of Sea Fury 162.

Naval Airman Farmer in the cockpit of Sea Fury 162 and Leading Pilot's Mate Peter Cook.

R. Neep

Winter conditions in the Yellow Sea. H.M.S. *Glory*.

R. Neep

Sea Fury dive bombing in North Korea.

R. Neep

Another bad landing on H.M.S. *Glory*.

A. F. Groom

Crash landing by a Fire Fly on H.M.S. *Glory*.

J. Weldrick

Main Headquarters of the Commonwealth Division was at Fort George, south of Pintail Bridge.

B. Gilding

The board bears the Commonwealth Division badge.

P. Bangs
Bren-gunner of 1st Bn. Duke of Wellington's Regiment in a front line trench.

P. Bangs
This is the Bren-gunner's view across the valley - no man's land - to the Chinese held hills opposite.

Peter Bangs, Duke of Wellington's Regiment, wearing the armoured waistcoat issued in 1952.

P. Bangs
Two porters of the Korean Service Corps in the front line trench of the Duke's.

R. Taylor
Korean "houseboys" with the Duke's. The boy on the left wears a Duke's beret and badge.

R. Taylor
A Korean who probably helped the cooks of the Duke's.

K. Keld

In March 1953, R.O.K.soldiers were integrated in all British battalions. They were dressed in D.W.R. uniform. From left: Kim Duk-Yong, D. Norton and Opan Suk.

A. Rouse

Lee Choul-Jo, Arthur Rouse, Lee Dong-Gin. 1st Battalion Royal Fusiliers, Camp Casey, March 1953.

R. Stevens
Brian Reece show, September or October 1951.

B. Hawkes
Ted Ray - "Ray's A Laugh" - with Helen Ward and Julie Shelley, October 1952.

I. T. Stratford

Carole Carr, September 1952.

I. T. Stratford

Carole Carr

Frankie Howerd show, November 1952. Probably Eve Boswell.

D. J. Hill, R.F.
Propaganda hung on front line wire calling on British soldiers to oppose the U.N. General Assembly decision not to automatically return all prisoners to China and North Korea if an armistice was agreed.

D. J. Hill, R.F.
Another banner hung on Royal Fusiliers' wire in December 1952. This one was a more emotional argument.

J. Weldrick
Globemaster at Kimpo airfield, Seoul. The normal transport for Tokyo leave.

J. Weldrick

Soldiers returning from Tokyo leave, Kimpo airfield.

J. Weldrick

Ginza Beer Hall, Tokyo.

D. Cope

Main H.Q., British Commonwealth Forces Korea, located in Kure, Japan.

H.M.T. *Empire Halladale*, one of many troopships which sailed between British ports and Pusan.

M.V. *Georgic*

British graves at the United Nations Cemetery near Pusan in 1981.

PART III

POEMS AND A SONG

KOREAN CHRISTMAS, 1950

Just what are we doing here?
Ice cold on a ridge in a foreign land,
Chilled by winds from the ends of the earth,
Far, very far from the homes we love,
Just what are we doing here?

The Korean peasant, gentle but strong,
Is swept up in a desperate fight;
His livelihood smashed by land engines of war,
Whilst death seeks him out from the skies.
Just what are we doing here?

Refugees trudge southwards below us,
With faltering, shuffling steps.
Do they know we are here to protect them,
That we hope they've the strength to survive?
Just what are we doing here?

In a Muscovite palace a tired tyrant sits,
Whose words mean these people must die.
A few hours more and their breath will be stilled,
But he'll never know, never care.
Just what are we doing here?

Someone, someday, must face up to his power
And say 'no' to that tyrant's greed.
Then peasant and wife can enjoy their old age;
Those of us who survive can go home.
That's what we are doing here!

A. E. Younger,
Major, Royal Engineers.

KOREA, 1951

Where the mighty ragged mountains
Rip the guts out of the sky,
And the desolation chills you
To the marrow of your bones.
Where the blinding drifting blizzards
Sear the unprotected eye,
And the biting bitter wind
Across the Yalu River moans.
A wild and savage landscape,
With its valleys grim and dreary...
Crag on wolfish crag, piled up, and
Glittering with the snows.
A harsh and brutal kingdom,
That would make an angel weary...
But your Scottish Soldier fought there,
And he knows...my God, he knows!

Ian E. Kaye,
The Black Watch and The Argyll and Sutherland Highlanders

I HAVE!

Have you known the lonely silence...
Not a bird-or-bug is stirring?
Your 'Mucker' lies there snoring
In his blankets at your side.
The dew drips off the Bren gun...
You can hear the damp grass growing;
And each squeak of your equipment
Is thunder, magnified!

Have you known the lonely silence...
At the witching-hour of midnight?
You've patted each grenade ten times,
And even whispered to your Sten...
Dozed-off - then woke in panic
With the fear of death upon you,
And every shape and shadow seems
Chock-full of 'little men'!

Have you known the lonely silence...
In the hour before the 'Stand-to'?
When every nerve is screaming
That there's Enemy around...
Then let your mess tins rattle,
Like a herd of berserk cattle...
Or stood and coughed (with hair on end!)
And shuddered at the sound?
I have!

Ian E. Kaye
The Black Watch and The Argyll and Sutherland Highlanders

AQUILA NON CAPIT MUSCAS: THE EAGLE DOES NOT CATCH FLIES

The Eagle does not catch flies!
But, have you seen the flies when the Eagle dies?
Fly-blown Fusiliers that the maggots eat;
No cool, English graveyard for them in their defeat.

In endless monotone they orchestrate; in curiosity and industry;
From living tissue to the dead; from the vomit of the dying and
The faeces soldier-made; on impulse, flitting from the food we eat;
inextricably attracted by dead and living things.

I pray to God that it is winter when I die! If not,
Bury me that day; leave me not in death sine die;
For mercy's sake, bury me before the stench arrives;
Leave not my once worn Eagle's body to the flies!

Ashley Cunningham-Boothe,
Royal Northumberland Fusiliers.

DEAR UGLY FRIEND, TOMMY MARTIN

Oh, Tommy Martin...oh, Tommy Martin,
I'll miss you - ugly, uncouth, fartin' Tommy Martin;
God, I'll miss you, Tommy Martin.

Oh, Tommy Martin...Oh, Tommy Martin,
Why did you let them kill you?
Stupid bastard, Tommy Martin!

Oh, Tommy Martin...Oh, Tommy Martin;
You know I loved you, ugly bastard;
Father, brother, best friend, Tommy Martin.

Oh, Tommy Martin...oh, Tommy Martin,
In your head you've gotta hole, Tommy Martin;
Shall I push your brains back, Tommy Martin?

Gotta hole in your head, and your dead, Tommy Martin,
Christ! you look untidy, now you're dead,
Tommy Martin...Tommy Martin.

Shall I let them wrap you up in; in your Soldier's
Blanket up in; what's the point: you're cold and dead,
Tommy Martin...Tommy Martin.

If I put you in a hole, there's no point;
Tommy Martin...Tommy Martin, for the 'Gooks' will dig
You up, for your blanket and your boots...
Tommy Martin.

God! I'm lonely now without you, Tommy Martin,
I am lonely now you've gone; I'm the frightened one;
I'm alone without you, Tommy Martin...I'm alone.

Oh, Tommy Martin...Fusilier Tommy Martin,
I won't let them bury you; for I've a need of you!
I'll pretend it hasn't happened; Tommy Martin I'm afraid.

Tommy Martin I am cold, its because I'm on my own;
If I live, I'll not forget you, Tommy Martin;
And if I die: I'll not be lonely...I've my friend...
Tommy Martin...Tommy Martin!

4453530 Corporal Thomas W. Martin was killed in hand-to-hand combat at Sibyon-ni, North Korea, serving with "W" Company 1st Bn. The Royal Northumberland Fusiliers, 1950.

Ashley Cunningham-Boothe,
Royal Northumberland Fusiliers.

ONE TIME OUT OF HISTORY'S CALENDAR

I had slept, not long, the soldier's fractured sleep,
That parked its arse upon the razor's edge of my taut nerves.
Dawn was not yet in the making in God's black opal eye.
Night coalesced the sky with the uncharitable earth and the
Inhospitable mountains,
Making one great, dreadful black of darkness.

Then, from my raw-ragged sleep, to stark-naked awakeness -
Mortar bombs ripped vulgar clutches from the earth's bone-dry crust,
And arms and legs - I wondered who had "bought it,"
in my instant-packaged hell,
As all around me cries of wounded Fusiliers gnawed
away at the edges of my sanity.

Peering out of the sparse sanctury of my hole's inside:
My eye travelled along snatches of tracers,
Busy sewing seams along the edges of the night's darkness,
Looking for a carcass to bury their bright lights in.

And flares which, in a grim imitation of illuminated revelling,
Mushroomed their brightness into the great, black cavern of the night;
Punctuated by gregarious, rattle-tattle sounds that battles
make about themselves.

Screaming, whistling, bugle-playing, Banzai-yelling 'Gooks' -
Like raving lunatics doing a demented Morris dance -
Reminding me of fireflies on a balmy summer's night,
Thrashed the obscene loops and strands of barbed-wire ignominy;
Halting long enough to be stilled by the Fusiliers Brens and Vickers.

Yet, still more came, and the more you shoot the Chinese,
The more there seems to be to shoot,
In a never-ending parody of insanely stupid, terribly worthless,
Quite courageous acts of raw courage.
Or was it opium, we asked?

When it comes to courage, which of you can separate the stupid
from the brave?
How can we take away from one soldier -
Because he serves the other side -
That which we would see as being nothing less than heroic in our own;
In battles so intense and infamous as to earn themselves a place in history,
Joining Battle Honours on a Regiment's Colours.

God forbid that you should spend one day of your life with the
'Shitdiggers' of the Infantry, writing history!

Ashley Cunningham-Boothe,
Royal Northumberland Fusiliers.

THE LAND OF THE MORNING CALM

So this is the Land of the Morning Calm!
Is this the Land of the Free?
No! this is the land where my soldiers have died,
in search of your Liberty.

Liberty viewed from a prisoner's cell
Shines brighter than previously;
And here is the land where my comrades are chained,
Whilst searching for your liberty.

We were conceived in liberty;
Conceived in the Land of the Free,
But its here in the Land of the Morning Calm
We discharge our freedom for thee.

Terry Moore,
April 1951,
1st Bn. The Royal Ulster Rifles.

THE FIELD OF CROSSES

The years have passed in plenty,
Since the time that I was there;
Along with countless others,
The burden for to share.

Now I often think of those who stayed,
Detained against their will,
'Neath a field of painted crosses,
On the side of a sun-baked hill.

What price the golden glory,
In the winning of the fight?
With you not here to share it,
But gone forever from our sight.

But you are not forgotten,
And this I remember, too,
But for the grace of God above,
I'd have shared that field with you.

Denis J. Woods,
Royal Artillery Signals.

THE WIRE

It is a new position:
We do not know exactly where 'they' are.
'They' are the enemy; and wiser now, for
They do not come in 'Banzai' charges any more;
they have learned new ways!
But, death is death, new ways or old,
And Death knows every trick in the book...
And, then some.
You sit on a sun-baked, shell-blasted hillside;
A score of telephone wires at your side,
And you trying each one in turn...
Identify, label, retain, discard.
All very boring, but vital!
You are an old hand at this game;
There are those who are not.
You are wise now in battle-lore;
There are those who are not.
You have learned quickly, but,
There are those who have not.
The work is slow...the day is hot;
Impatience is the Corporal's name.
And, at his age, rank is all-powerful...
Even against reason!
'Impatience' takes a line and
Begins to walk down the forward slope.
Forward, to where 'they' might be.
Reason tries its hand again...
But rank is all-powerful!
You point to the wire...
And the little, red triangles;
Death lurks beyond!
But, 'Impatience' ignores you, and
The signs which scream: MINES!
'Impatience' now tells you that where
There's a line, there is also a path,
Else, 'how could they lay the line?'
Ten paces past the wire 'Impatience' is dead!
Blown to shreds by a mine that 'they' had put there...
After the line was laid...!

Denis J. Woods,
Royal Artillery Signals.

KIM HO HAN

In this country that we're in, though you may get jeeps for gin,
And we may ride in style along the tracks;
There are hills so bloomin' steep, you can't get up in a jeep,
And rations must be humped on people's backs.

So the brainy brass hats at long last saw
The need to form the Korean Service Corps;
Our chief porter was a man by the name of Kim Ho Han,
Who arrived, complete with rice bowl, dressed in blue.

It was Han! Han! Han! - come hurry with that can,
We can't 'brew' cause we've no water,
Where's that sweating, stumbling porter?
That squint-eyed yellow idol, Kim Ho Han.

Our first task in the fight, was to capture 358,
And for half a day we staggered up the scrub;
When the top was just in sight, we dug in for the night,
And every man's first thought was of his grub.
With the Kiwis at our rear, and the Chinese Reds quite near,
Still thinking of his rations, every man;
When stumbling up the track, with his 'A' Frame on his back,
Came good old grinning, grunting, Kim Ho Han.

It was Han! Han! Han! look gillo with that can,
Balli, Balli, Idewha - or we'll never get our char,
You Kimchi - breathing pagan,
Kim Ho Han.

When the rain came down in torrent,
Leaving mud so deep I'll warrant,
That most of us were stuck up to our knees;
But the porters still got through -
Carrying grub and ammo too,
And smiled, 'neath sweat-stained brows, as though with ease.

So its Han! Han! Han! though your yellow hide we'd tan,
I'd not carry ten men's rations, in your human packmule fashion,
You've done us loyal service, we thank you Kim Ho Han.

Neville Faulkener

MOVING ON

Perhaps the only original British soldier's song to emerge in Korea was "Moving On", which had an infinite variety of verses. These are some refined but evocative ones.

There's plenty of food from Uncle Sam
Corn beef hash, lima beans and ham.
(Chorus) We're moving on, yes, we'll soon be gone;
When you hit Pusan, don't cause a jam,
'Cos we're moving on.

See the Chinkies coming up "355"
The Yanks pulling out in overdrive
(Chorus) We're saying good-bye to the rest of the guys,
And we're moving on, yes, we'll soon be gone.

If you go on R and R
Tokyo is not so far.
(Chorus)

Ashes to ashes, dust to dust
If the Chinkies don't get you, then Asahi must.
(Chorus)

If you go down to old Inchon
All you'll need is plenty of Won.
(Chorus)

See the Chinkies coming over the ridge
Heading like hell for Pintail bridge.
(Chorus).

The chorus had many versions, for example:

Here comes Poppasan down the track
With a twenty-five pounder on his back;
We're moving on, to old Tokchon.

(Chorus) When you get to Tokchon
Don't cause a jam,
'Cos we're moving on
To sweet Suwon.

Appendix one

UNITED KINGDOM FORCES IN THE KOREAN THEATRE OF WAR.

Armour	**Period of Service**
8 King's Royal Irish Hussars	November 1950 - December 1951
"C" Squadron, 7th Royal Tank Regiment	November 1950 - October 1951
5 Royal Inniskilling Dragoon Guards	December 1951 - December 1952
1 Royal Tank Regiment	December 1952 - December 1953

Royal Artillery	
45 Field Regiment	November 1950 - November 1951
11 (Sphinx) Independent Light A.A. Battery (converted to 4.2 Mortars in June, 1951)	November 1950 - November 1951
170 Independent Mortar Battery	November 1950 - October 1951
14 Field Regiment	November 1951 - December 1952
120 Light A.A. Battery	October 1951. Joined 61st Light Regiment in December 1952
42 Light A.A. Battery, (Redesignated 42nd Light Battery in January 1952)	November 1951. Joined 61st Light Regiment in February 1952
15 Location Battery	
61 Light Regiment	January 1952 - January 1954
20 Field Regiment	December 1952 - December 1953
74 Medium Battery	February 1953 - November 1953

Infantry	
1 Bn. The Middlesex Regiment	August 1950 - May 1951
1 Bn. The Argyll and Sutherland Highlanders	August 1950 - April 1951
1 Bn. The Royal Northumberland Fusiliers	November 1950 - October 1951
1 Bn. The Gloucestershire Regiment	November 1950 - November 1951
1 Bn. The Royal Ulster Rifles	November 1950 - October 1951
1 Bn. King's Own Scottish Borderers	April 1951 - August 1952
1 Bn. The King's Shropshire Light Infantry	May 1951 - September 1952
1 Bn. The Royal Norfolk Regiment	October 1951 - September 1952
1 Bn. The Royal Leicestershire Regiment	October 1951 - June 1952
1 Bn. The Welch Regiment	November 1951 - November 1952
1 Bn. The Black Watch	June 1952 - July 1953
1 Bn. The Royal Fusiliers (City of London Regiment)	August 1952 - August 1953
1 Bn. The Durham Light Infantry	September 1952 - September 1953
1 Bn. The King's Regiment	September 1952 - October 1953
1 Bn. The Duke of Wellington's Regiment	October 1952 - November 1953
1 Bn. The Royal Scots	July 1953 - May 1954

Royal Engineers	**Period of Service**
55 Field Squadron	November 1950. Joined 28th Field Engineer Regiment July 1951
12 Field Squadron	1951 -
28 Field Engineer Regiment (Commonwealth integrated unit)	July 1951 - 1955
64 Field Park Squadron (Commonwealth integrated unit)	July 1951 - 1955
206 Army Postal Unit	
28 Field Engineer Regiment (Commonwealth integrated unit)	July 1951 - 1955
64 Field Park Squadron (Commonwealth integrated unit)	July 1951 - 1955
Royal Signals	
27 Brigade Signals Troop	
29 Brigade Signals Troop	
Commonwealth Division Signals Regiment (Commonwealth integrated unit)	July 1951 - 1955
Royal Army Medical Corps	
Included:	
26 Field Ambulance	December 1950 - 1954
Commonwealth General Hospital, Kure, Japan. (Commonwealth integrated unit)	
Communications Zone Medical Unit (Commonwealth integrated unit)	September 1952 - December 1954

Royal Army Dental Corps

Queen Alexandra's Royal Army Nursing Corps

Royal Army Service Corps
Included:
57 Company
78 Company
76 Supply Company
37 Field Bakery Platoon
39 Field Bakery Platoon

Royal Electrical and Mechanical Engineers
Included:
10 Infantry Workshops
11 Infantry Workshops
16 Infantry Workshops

Royal Army Ordnance Corps

Intelligence Corps
Included:
904 Field Security Section
104 Army Photographic Interpretation Section

Royal Military Police
Included:
27 Brigade Provost Section
28 Brigade Provost Section
Commonwealth Division Provost Company
(Commonwealth integrated unit)

Royal Army Pay Corps
Included:
73 Forward Base Pay Office
204 Field Cash Office

Navy Army Air/Force Institutes/Expeditionary Forces Institute

2 Public Relations Service

II. ROYAL AIR FORCE

Far East Air Force Flying Boat Wing
Far East Air Force Transport Wing
1903 Army Observation Post Flight
1913 Light Liaison Flight

III. ROYAL MARINES

Included:
41 Independent Commando

IV. ROYAL NAVY

Headquarters ships	**Period of Service**
Ladybird	September 1950 - April 1953
Tyne	April - July 1953
Light Fleet Carriers	
Unicorn	July 1950 - July 1953
Triumph (800; 827 Squadron)	July 1950 - September 1950
Theseus (807, 810 Squadron)	October 1950 - April 1951
Glory (804, 812 Squadron; 801, 821 Squadron)	April - September 1951 January - May 1952 November 1952 - May 1953
Ocean (802, 825 Squadron; 807, 810 Squadron)	May - October 1952 May - July 1953

Cruisers	Period of Service
Belfast	June - August 1950 January 1951 - September 1952
Jamaica	June - October 1950
Kenya	July 1950 - August 1951
Ceylon	August 1950 - July 1952
Newcastle	July 1952 - July 1953
Birmingham	September 1952 - July 1953

Destroyers	
Charity	July 1950 - January 1951 July - September 1951 December 1951 - March 1952 August - November 1952 February - April 1953 June - July 1953
Cockade	July - November 1950 March - August 1951 October - December 1951 January - March 1952 December 1952 - February 1953 April - July 1953
Comus	July - November 1950 March - August 1951 October - December 1951 May - September 1952 November 1952 - February 1953
Concord	September 1950 - January 1951 April - May 1951 August - November 1951 January - April 1952 July - August 1952 May - July 1953
Consort	June 1950 - April 1951 June - September 1951 May - August 1952 November 1952 - February 1953 March - May 1953
Constance	October 1950 - March 1951 June - July 1951 November 1951 - February 1952 June - December 1952
Cossack	June 1950 - October 1951 February - May 1952 July 1952 September 1952 - January 1953 May - July 1953

Frigates	Period of Service
Alacrity	June - August 1950 February - June 1951 December 1951 - February 1952
Alert	August - October 1950 October 1951
Amethyst	February - June 1951 September 1951 - January 1952 April - July 1952
Black Swan	June - August 1950 February - June 1951 September - November 1951
Cardigan Bay	November 1950 - January 1951 June - September 1951 January - April 1952 June - September 1952 January - July 1953
Crane	March - June 1952 August - September 1952 November 1952 - March 1953 July 1953
Hart	June - August 1950 February - March 1951
Modeste	April - July 1953
Morecambe Bay	October 1950 - January 1951 June - September 1951 March - May 1952 August - November 1952 May - July 1953
Mounts Bay	August - November 1950 December 1950 - January 1951 June - September 1951 December 1951 - April 1952 June - November 1952 March - June 1953
Opossum	November 1952 - April 1953
St. Bride's Bay	December 1950 - January 1951 August - December 1951 July - October 1952 April - June 1953
Sparrow	December 1952 - February 1953 April - June 1953
Whitesand Bay	August - December 1950 June - July 1951 October 1951 - February 1952 April - July 1953

Fleet Train. Royal Fleet Auxiliary	Period of Service
Maine (Hospital Ship Company included Queen Alexandra's Royal Naval Nursing Service)	June 1950 - February 1952 May 1952 - July 1953
Fort Charlotte (Naval and Victualling Stores Issuing Ship)	
Fort Rosalie (Armament Store Issuing Ship)	
Fort Langley	
Fort Sandusky	
Choysang (Merchant Fleet Auxiliary Armament Store Issuing Ship)	
Echodale (Oiler)	
Green Ranger (Oiler)	
Brown Ranger (Oiler)	
Wave Chief (Oiler)	
Wave Conqueror (Oiler)	
Wave Knight (Oiler)	
Wave Laird (Oiler)	
Wave Premier (Oiler)	
Wave Prince (Oiler)	
Wave Regent (Oiler)	
Wave Sovereign (Oiler)	

Appendix two

ARMY UNITS IN THE PEACEKEEPING FORCES 1953 - 1957.

Armour	**Period of Service**
5 Royal Tank Regiment	December 1953 - December 1954
Royal Artillery	
42 Field Regiment	1954
19 Field Regiment	1955
48 Field Regiment	1955-56
98 Medium Battery	1954
Infantry	
1 Bn. The Essex Regiment	August 1953 - June 1954
1 Bn. The Royal Warwickshire Regiment	September 1953 - June 1954
1 Bn. The King's Own Royal Regiment	October 1953 - September 1954
1 Bn. The North Staffordshire Regiment	November 1953 - September 1954
1 Bn. The Northamptonshire Regiment	July - December 1954
1 Bn. The Royal Irish Fusiliers	June - November 1954
1 Bn. The Dorset Regiment	August 1954 - August 1955
1 Bn. The Queen's Own Cameron Highlanders	August 1955 - June 1956
1 Bn. The Royal Sussex Regiment	August 1956 - July 1957

Royal Engineers

Royal Army Service Corps

Royal Electrical and Mechanical Engineers

Royal Army Ordnance Corps

Royal Military Police

Royal Army Educational Corps

Appendix three

AWARDS OF THE VICTORIA CROSS AND GEORGE CROSS. CITATIONS OF UNITS BY THE PRESIDENT OF THE UNITED STATES AND BY THE PRESIDENT OF THE REPUBLIC OF KOREA.

THE VICTORIA CROSS

MAJOR KENNETH MUIR (50980)

The Argyll and Sutherland Highlanders (Princess Louise's)

(Posthumous)

On 23 September, 1950, "B" and "C" Companies of the 1st Battalion The Argyll and Sutherland Highlanders attacked an enemy-held feature, Hill 282, and by 0800 hrs. had consolidated upon it.

Some difficulty was experienced in evacuating the wounded from the position and demands were made for stretcher-bearing parties to be sent forward by the Battalion. At this juncture the position came under mortar and shell fire.

At approximately 0900 hrs. a stretcher-bearing party arrived and with it came the Battalion Second-in-Command, Major K. Muir. He proceeded to organize the evacuation of the casualties.

At approximately 0930 hrs. small parties of the enemy started to infiltrate on the left flank necessitating the reinforcing of the forward platoon. For the next hour this infiltration increased, as did the shelling and mortaring, causing further casualties within the two companies.

By 1100 hrs. casualties were moderately severe and some difficulty was being experienced in holding the enemy. In addition, due to reinforcing the left flank and to providing personnel to assist with the wounded, both companies were so inextricably mixed that it was obvious that they must come under a unified command. Major Muir, although only visiting the position, automatically took over command and with complete disregard for his own personal safety started to move around the forward elements, cheering on and encouraging the men to greater efforts despite the fact that ammunition was running low. He was continually under enemy fire, and, despite entreaties from officers and men alike, refused to take cover.

An air-strike against the enemy was arranged and air recognition panels were put out on the ground. At approximately 1215 hrs. the air-strike came in, but unfortunately the aircraft hit the companies' position instead of that of the enemy. The main defensive position was hit with fire bombs and machine-gun fire, causing more casualties and necessitating the withdrawal of the remaining troops to a position some fifty feet below the crest. There is no doubt that a complete retreat from the hill would have been fully justified at this time. Only some thirty fighting men remained and ammunition was extremely low. Major Muir, however, realized that the enemy had not taken immediate advantage of the unfortunate incident and that the crest was still unoccupied although under fire.

With the assistance of the three remaining officers, he immediately formed a small force of some thirty all ranks and personally led a counter-attack on the crest. To appreciate fully the implication of this, it is necessary to realize how demoralizing the effect of the air-strike had been and it was entirely due to the courage, determination and splendid example of this officer that such a counter-attack was possible. All ranks responded magnificently and the crest was retaken.

From this moment on, Major Muir's actions were beyond all possible praise. He was determined that the wounded would have adequate time to be taken out and he was just as determined that the enemy would not take the crest. Grossly outnumbered and under heavy automatic fire, Major Muir moved about his small force, redistributing fast diminishing ammunition, and when the ammunition for his own weapon was spent he took over a 2-inch mortar, which he used with very great effect against the enemy. While firing the mortar he was still shouting encouragements and advice to his men, and for a further five minutes the enemy were held. Finally, Major Muir was hit with two bursts of automatic fire which mortally wounded him, but even then he retained consciousness and was still as determined to fight on. His last words were: "The Gooks will never drive the Argylls off this hill."

The effect of his splendid leadership on the men was nothing short of amazing and it was entirely due to his magnificent courage and example and the spirit which he imbued in those about him that all wounded were evacuated from the hill, and, as was subsequently discovered, very heavy casualties inflicted on the enemy in the defence of the crest. - *London Gazette, 5th January, 1951.*

LIEUTENANT-COLONEL JAMES POWER CARNE, D.S.O. (33647)
The Gloucestershire Regiment

On the night 22nd/23rd April, 1951, Lieutenant-Colonel Carne's battalion, 1 Glosters, was heavily attacked and the enemy on the Imjin River were repulsed, having suffered heavy casualties. On 23rd, 24th April, 1951, the Battalion was heavily and incessantly engaged by vastly superior numbers of enemy, who repeatedly launched mass attacks, but were stopped at close quarters.

During the 24th and 25th April, 1951, the Battalion was completely cut off from the rest of the Brigade, but remained a fighting entity, in face of almost continual onslaughts from an enemy who were determined, at all costs and regardless of casualties, to over-run it. Throughout, Lieutenant-Colonel Carne's manner remained coolness itself, and on the wireless, the only communication he still had with Brigade, he repeatedly assured the Brigade Commander that all was well with his Battalion, that they could hold on and that everyone was in good heart.

Throughout the entire engagement, Lieutenant-Colonel Carne, showing a complete disregard for his own safety, moved among the whole Battalion under very heavy mortar and machine-gun fire, inspiring the utmost confidence and the will to resist, amongst his troops.

On two separate occasions, armed with a rifle and grenades, he personally led assault parties which drove back the enemy and saved important situations.

Lieutenant-Colonel Carne's example of courage, coolness and leadership was felt not only in his own Battalion, but throughout the whole Brigade.

He fully realized that his flanks had been turned, but he also knew that the abandonment of his position would clear the way for the enemy to make a major break-through and this would have endangered the Corps.

When at last it was apparent that his Battalion would not be relieved and on orders from higher authority, he organized his Battalion into small, officer-led parties, who then broke out, whilst he himself in charge of a small party fought his way out, but was captured within twenty-four hours.

Lieutenant-Colonel Carne showed powers of leadership which can seldom have been surpassed in the history of our Army.

He inspired his officers and men to fight beyond the normal limits of human endurance, in spite of overwhelming odds and ever-increasing casualties, shortage of ammunition and of water. - *London Gazette, 27th October, 1953*

LIEUTENANT PHILIP KENNETH EDWARD CURTIS (365680)

The Duke of Cornwall's Light Infantry,
attached The Gloucestershire Regiment
(Posthumous)

During the first phase of the Battle of the Imjin River on the night of 22nd/23rd April, 1951, "A" Company, 1 Glosters, was heavily attacked by a large enemy force. By dawn on 23rd April, the enemy had secured a footing on the "Castle Hill" site in very close proximity to No. 2 Platoon's position. The Company Commander ordered No. 1 Platoon, under the command of Lieutenant Curtis, to carry out a counter-attack with a view to dislodging the enemy from the position. Under the covering fire of medium machine guns, the counter attack, gallantly led by Lieutenant Curtis, gained initial success, but was eventually held up by heavy fire and grenades. Enemy from just below the crest of the hill were rushed to reinforce the position and a fierce fire-fight developed, grenades also being freely used by both sides in this close-quarter engagement. Lieutenant Curtis ordered some of his men to give him covering fire while he himself rushed the main position of resistance; in this charge Lieutenant Curtis was severely wounded by a grenade. Several of his men crawled out and pulled him back under cover, but, recovering himself, Lieutenant Curtis insisted on making a second attempt. Breaking free from the men who wished to restrain him, he made another desperate charge, hurling grenades as he went, but was killed by a burst of fire when within a few yards of his objective.

Although the immediate objective of this counter-attack was not achieved, it had yet a great effect on the subsequent course of the battle; for although the enemy had gained a footing on a position vital to the defence of the whole company area, the success had resulted in such a furious reaction that they made no further effort to exploit their success in this immediate area; had they done so, the eventual withdrawal of the company might well have proved impossible.

Lieutenant Curtis's conduct was magnificent throughout this bitter battle. - *London Gazette, 1st December, 1953.*

14471590 PRIVATE WILLIAM SPEAKMAN

Black Watch (Royal Highland Regiment), attached to the 1st Battalion The King's Own Scottish Borderers

From 0400 hrs., 4th November 1951, the defensive positions held by 1st Battalion The King's Own Scottish Borderers were continuously subjected to heavy and accurate enemy shell and mortar fire. At 1545 hrs., this fire became intense and continued thus for the next two hours, considerably damaging the defences and wounding a number of men.

At 1645 hrs. the enemy in their hundreds advanced in wave upon wave against the King's Own Scottish Borderers' positions, and by 1745 hrs. fierce hand-to-hand fighting was taking place on every position.

Private Speakman, a member of "B" Company, Headquarters, learning that the section holding the left shoulder of the company's position had been seriously depleted by casualties, had had its N.C.Os. wounded and was being over-run, decided on his own initiative to drive the enemy off the position and keep them off it. To effect this he collected quickly a pile of grenades and a party of six men. Then, displaying complete disregard for his own personal saftey, he led his party in a series of grenade charges against the enemy; and continued doing so as each successive wave of enemy reached the crest of the hill. The force and determination of his charges broke up each successive enemy onslaught and resulted in an ever-mounting pile of enemy dead.

Having led some ten charges, through withering enemy machine-gun and mortar fire, Private Speakman was eventually severely wounded in the leg. Undaunted by his wounds, he continued to lead charge after charge against the enemy, and it was only after a direct order from his superior officer that he agreed to pause for a first field dressing to be applied to his wounds. Having had his wounds bandaged, Private Speakman immediately joined his comrades and led them again and again forward in a series of grenade charges, up to the time of the withdrawal of his company at 2100 hrs.

At the critical moment of the withdrawal, amidst an inferno of enemy machine-gun and mortar fire, as well as grenades, Private Speakman led a final charge to clear the crest of the hill and hold it, whilst the remainder of his company withdrew. Encouraging his gallant but by now sadly depleted party, he assailed the enemy with showers of grenades and kept them at bay sufficiently long for his company to effect its withdrawal.

Under the stress and strain of this battle, Private Speakman's outstanding powers of leadership were revealed, and he so dominated the situation that he inspired his comrades to stand firm and fight the enemy to a standstill.

His great gallantry and utter contempt for his own personal safety were an inspiration to all his comrades. He was, by his heroic actions, personally responsible for causing enormous losses to the enemy, assisting his company to maintain their position for some four hours and saving the lives of many of his comrades when they were forced to withdraw from their position.

Private Speakman's heroism under intense fire throughout the operation and when painfully wounded was beyond praise and is deserving of supreme recognition. *- London Gazette, 28th December, 1951.*

GEORGE CROSS

22105517 Fusilier Derek Godfrey Kinne
The Royal Northumberland Fusiliers

In August, 1950, Fusilier Kinne volunteered for service in Korea. He joined the 1st Battalion The Royal Northumberland Fusiliers, and was captured by Chinese Communist forces on 25th April, 1951, the last day of the Imjin River battle. From then on he had only two objects in mind: firstly to escape, and secondly by his contempt for his captors and their behaviour, and his utter disregard for the treatment meted out to him, to raise the morale of his fellow-prisoners. The treatment which he received during his period of captivity is summarized in the succeeding paragraphs.

Fusilier Kinne escaped for the first time within 24 hours of capture, but was retaken a few days later while attempting to regain our own lines. Eventually he rejoined a large group of prisoners being marched north to prison camps, and despite the hardships of this march, which lasted a month, rapidly emerged as a man of outstanding leadership and very high morale. His conduct was a fine example to all his fellow-prisoners.

In July, 1952, Fusilier Kinne, who was by now well known to his captors, was accused by them of being non-co-operative and was brutally interrogated about the other P.W. who had unco-operative views. As a result of his refusal to inform on his comrades, and for striking back at a Chinese officer who assaulted him, he was twice severely beaten up and tried up for periods of 12 and 24 hours, being made to stand on tip-toe with a running noose round his neck which would throttle him if he attempted to relax in any way.

He escaped on 27th July, but was recaptured two days later. He was again beaten up very severely, and placed in handcuffs (which could be and frequently were tightened so as to restrict circulation), from which he was not released until 16th October, 1952, a period of 81 days.

He was accused of insincerity, a hostile attitude towards the Chinese, "sabotage" of compulsory political study, escape, and of being reactionary. From 15th to 20th August he was confined in a very small box cell, where he was made to sit to attention all day, being periodically beaten, prodded with bayonets, kicked and spat upon by the guards, and denied any washing facilities.

On 20th August 1952, he was made to stand to attention for seven hours and when he complained was beaten by the Chinese guard commander with the butt of a submachine gun, which eventually went off and killed the guard commander. For this Fusilier Kinne was beaten senseless with belts and bayonets, stripped of his clothes, and thrown into a dank rat-infested hole until 19th September. He was frequently taken out and beaten, including once (on 16th September) with pieces of planking until he was unconscious.

On 16th October Fusilier Kinne was tried by a Chinese military court for escape and for being a reactionary and hostile to the Chinese, and was sentenced to twelve months solitary confinement. This was increased to eighteen months when he complained at his trial of denial of medical attention, including that for a severe double hernia which he had sustained in June, 1952, while trying to escape.

On 5th December, 1952, he was transferred to a special penal company. His last award of solitary confinement was on 2nd June, 1953, when he was sentenced for defying Chinese orders and wearing a rosette in celebration of Coronation Day.

He was eventually exchanged at Panmunjom on 10th August, 1953. As late as 8th and 9th August he was threatened with non-repatriation for demanding an interview with the International Red Cross Representatives who were visiting prisoner-of-war camps.

Fusilier Kinne was during the course of his periods of solitary confinement kept in no less than seven different places of imprisonment, including a security police gaol, under conditions of the most extreme degradation and increasing brutality. Every possible method both physical and mental was employed by his captors to break his spirit, a task which proved utterly beyond their powers. Latterly he must have been fully aware that every time he flaunted his captors and showed openly his detestation of themselves and their methods he was risking his life. He was in fact several times threatened with death or non-repatriation. Nevertheless he was always determined to show that he was prepared neither to be intimidated nor cowed by brutal treatment at the hands of a barbarous enemy.

His powers of resistance and his determination to oppose and fight the enemy to the maximum were beyond praise. His example was an inspiration to all ranks who came into contact with him. - *London Gazette, 13th April, 1954.*

LIEUTENANT TERENCE EDWARD WATERS (463718)
The West Yorkshire Regiment (The Prince of Wales's Own), attached The Gloucestershire Regiment
(Posthumous)

Lieutenant Waters was captured subsequent to the Battle of the Imjin River, 22nd-25th April, 1951. By this time he had sustained a serious wound in the top of the head and yet another most painful wound in the arm as a result of this action.

On the journey to Pyongyang with other captives, he set a magnificent example of courage and fortitude in remaining with wounded other ranks on the march, whom he felt it his duty to care for to the best of his ability.

Subsequently, after a journey of immense hardship and privation, the party arrived at an area west of Pyongyang adjacent to P.W. Camp 12 and known generally as "The Caves," in which they were held captive. They found themselves imprisoned in a tunnel driven into the side of a hill through which a stream of water flowed continuously, flooding a great deal of the floor in which were packed a great number of South Korean and European prisoners of war in rags, filthy, crawling with lice. In this cavern a number died daily from wounds sickness, or merely malnutrition: they fed on two small meals of boiled maize daily. Of medical attention there was none.

Lieutenant Waters appreciated that few, if any, of his numbers would survive these conditions, in view of their weakness and the absolute lack of attention for their wounds. After a visit from a North Korean Political Officer, who attempted to persuade them to volunteer to join a prisoner-of-war group known as "Peace Fighters" (that is, active participants in the propaganda movement against their own side) with a promise of better food, of medical treatment and other amenities as a reward for such activity - an offer that was refused unanimously - he decided to order his men to pretend to accede to the offer in an effort to save their lives. This he did, giving the necessary instructions to the senior other rank with the British party, Sergeant Hoper, that the men would go upon his order without fail.

Whilst realizing that this act would save the lives of his party, he refused to go himself, aware that the task of maintaining British prestige was vested in him.

Realizing that they had failed to subvert an officer with the British party, the North Koreans now made a series of concerted efforts to persuade Lieutenant Waters to save himself by joining the camp. This he steadfastly refused to do. He died a short time after.

He was a young, inexperienced officer, comparatively recently commissioned from the Royal Military Academy Sandhurst, yet he set an example of the highest gallantry. -*London Gazette, 13th April, 1954.*

THE DISTINGUISHED UNIT CITATION (UNITED STATES)

The Distinguished Unit Citation is awarded by the President of the United States to the Army

General Order No. 286 of the Eighth United States Army Korea (EUSAK) dated 8th May 1951.

The 1st Battalion The Gloucestershire Regiment, British Army and C Troop, 107th Independent Mortar Battery, Royal Artillery, attached, are cited for exceptionally outstanding performance of duty and extraordinary heroism in action against the armed enemy near Solma-ri Korea, on the 23rd, 24th and 25th April 1951. The 1st Battalion and C Troop were defending a very critical sector of the battle front during a determined attack by the enemy. The defending units were overwhelmingly outnumbered. The 83rd Chinese Communist Army drove the full force of its savage assault at the positions held by the 1st Battalion Gloucestershire Regiment and attached unit. The route of supply ran southeast from the battalion between two hills. The hills dominated the surrounding terrain northwest to the Imjin River. Enemy pressure built up on the battalion front during the day 23rd April. On the 24th April the weight of the attack had driven the right flank of the battalion back. The pressure grew heavier and heavier and the battalion and attached unit were forced into a perimeter defence on Hill 235. During the night heavy enemy forces had by-passed the staunch defenders and closed all avenues of escape. The courageous soldiers of the battalion and attached unit were holding the critical route selected by the enemy for one column of the general offensive designed to encircle and destroy I Corps. These gallant soldiers would not retreat. As they were compressed tighter in their perimeter defence, they called for close air strikes to assist in holding firm. Completely surrounded by tremendous numbers, these indomitable, resolute, and tenacious soldiers fought back with unsurpassed fortitude and courage. As ammunition ran low and the advancing hordes moved closer and closer these splendid soldiers fought back viciously to prevent the enemy from overrunning the position and moving rapidly to the south. Their heroic stand provided the critically needed time to regroup other I Corps units and block the southern advance of the enemy. Time and again efforts were made to reach the battalion, but the enemy strength blocked each effort. Without thought of defeat or surrender, this heroic force demonstrated superb battlefield courage and discipline. Every yard of ground they surrendered was covered with enemy dead until the last gallant soldier of the fighting Battalion was overpowered by the final surge of the enemy masses. The 1st Battalion The Gloucestershire Regiment and C Troop, 107th Independent Mortar Battery displayed such gallantry, determination, and esprit de corps in accomplishing their mission under extremely difficult and hazardous conditions so as to set them apart and above other units participating in the same battle. Their sustained brilliance in battle, their resoluteness, and extraordinary heroism are in keeping with the finest traditions of the renowned military forces of the British Commonwealth, and reflect unsurpassed credit on these courageous soldiers and their homeland.

By Command of Lieutenant General Van Fleet.

PRESIDENTIAL UNIT CITATION

United States

The Presidential Unit Citation is awarded by the President of the United States to the Navy. The Citation was awarded in May 1953 to the "First Marine Division, Reinforced". The 41st Independent Commando, Royal Marines, was not then listed among the reinforcing units owing to regulations excluding the award to foreign units. But by Executive Order 10694 of 10th January 1957 this restriction was abolished and 41st Commando was added to the Citation under the new heading "Attached Foreign Units".

Citation:

For extraordinary heroism and outstanding performance of duty in action against enemy aggressor forces in the Chosin Reservoir and Koto-ri area of Korea from 27th November to 11th December 1950. When the full fury of the enemy counterattack struck both the Eighth Army and the Tenth Corps on 27th and 28th November 1950, the First Marine Division, Reinforced, operating as the left flank division of the Tenth Corps, launched a daring assault westward from Yudam-ni in an effort to cut the road and rail communications of hostile forces attacking the Eighth Army and, at the same time, continued its mission of protecting a vital main supply route consisting of a tortuous mountain road running southward to Chinhung-ni, approximately thirty-five miles distant. Ordered to withdraw to Hamhung in company with attached army and other friendly units in the face of tremendous pressure in the Chosin Reservoir area, the Division began an epic battle against the bulk of the enemy Third Route Army and, while small intermediate garrisons at Hagaru-ri and Koto-ri held firmly against repeated and determined attacks by hostile forces, gallantly fought its way successively to Hagaru-ri, Koto-ri, Chinhung-ni and Hamhung over twisting, mountainous and icy roads in sub-zero temperatures. Battling desperately night and day in the face of almost insurmountable odds throughout a period of two weeks of intense and sustained combat, the First Marine Division, Reinforced, emerged from its ordeal as a fighting unit with its wounded, with its guns and equipment and with its prisoners, decisively defeating seven enemy divisions, together with elements of three others, and inflicting major losses which seriously impared the military effectiveness of the hostile forces for a considerable period of time. The valiant fighting spirit, relentless perseverance and heroic fortitude of the officers and men of the First Marine Division, Reinforced, in battle against vastly outnumbering enemy, were in keeping with the highest traditions of the United States Naval Service.

PRESIDENTIAL UNIT CITATION

Republic of Korea

The two Citations, here translated, were awarded by the President of the Republic of Korea, Syngman Rhee.

1. The President of the Republic of Korea takes profound pleasure in citing for outstanding and heroic performance of duty on the field of battle during the period of 5th September - 15th September, 1950. The 27th British Infantry Brigade for the Award of The Presidential Unit Citation.

   For holding a critical sector of the Naktong river line during the height of the enemy's attack, and for its participation in the general offensive of 16th September in which it crossed the Naktong river and attacked toward Kumchon.

   This marked and brilliant performance of duty by each individual member of the 27th British Infantry Brigade is in accord with the highest traditions of military service.

   This citation carries with it the right to wear the Presidential Unit Citation Ribbon by each individual of the 27th British Infantry Brigade which served in Korea in the stated period.

2. The President of the Republic of Korea takes profound pleasure in citing for exceptionally meritorious service and heroism during the period 19th February 1951 through 31st July 1951 H.M. Hospital Ship *Maine* for the award of the Presidential Unit Citation.

   H.M.H.S. *Maine* has distinguished itself in support of U.N. forces in Korea by providing expert and humanitarian care for friendly forces. This vessel provided medical and surgical care and consultative service in the cases of many Republic of Korea war casualties many of whom were selected cases requiring unusual or particularly difficult types of medical treatment. The *Maine,* therefore contributed greatly to the morale of the Army and of the people of Korea by the assurance of the most modern and effective types of medical care known to science in the many particular instances where they were required. The Medical Officers of H.M.H.S. *Maine* through extra effort over and above their already strenuous and full occupation in regularly assigned duties gave unstintingly of their remaining time, in visiting Republic of Korea hospitals and medical installations, and rendering instructive and consultative service which did much to improve the knowledge and ability of the Korean doctors in the care and administration of war casualties.

   The activities of the Hospital Ship, founded in the motives of alleviating the suffering caused by war, and improving medical care as well as the highly substantial and beneficial effect in the recovery of casualties for further service, served in a great degree beyond the call of duty of its personnel, in the establishment and cementing of friendly relations between the Government of the Republic of Korea and Great Britain, and providing an unusually high humanitarian as well as military contribution to the success of the war objectives of the Republic of Korea. The outstanding performance of duty by each individual member of H.M.H.S. *Maine* is in accord with the highest traditions of military service.

Appendix four

SELECT CHRONOLOGY.

Before the Korean War

1910 : Korea annexed to the Japanese Empire.

1945

15 August	Surrender of Japan. President Truman issued a General Order dividing Korea at the 38th parallel to allow Soviet and American occupying forces to disarm the Japanese.
24 August	Soviet troops completed occupation of Northern half of Korea.
8 September	American occupation forces arrived in Korea.
27 November	The USA, USSR and UK signed the Moscow Agreement proposing a four-power trusteeship for Korea. (By 1947, there had been no agreement about how to carry it out.)

1947

14 November	The UN General Assembly established the UN Temporary Commission on Korea (UNTCOK) and resolved that if should supervise a general election.

1948

12 January	UNTCOK convened in Seoul.
23 January	The Soviet occupation forces excluded UNTCOK from North Korea.
10 May	UNTCOK supervised a General Election held in South Korea.
17 July	The Constitution of the Republic of Korea was promulgated.
15 August	The Government of the Republic of Korea was formed.
12 December	The UN General Assembly recognised the Government of the Republic of Korea as the only lawful Government in Korea, and created a permanent UN Commision on Korea (UNCOK).
26 December	Soviet troops completed their evacuation of Korea.

1949

	The USA, Britain, Canada, New Zealand and Australia recognised the Republic of Korea.
29 June	American occupation forces completed their evacuation of Korea.

1950

9-23 June	UNCOK Military Observers field trip along 38th parallel. Their report, drafted 24th June, noted that the South Korean army is "organised entirely for defence and is in no condition to carry out an attack on a large scale against the forces of the North."

The Korean War

1950

25 June	: North Korean forces invaded South Korea without warning.
26 June	: The UN Security Council condemned the attack by North Korea as an assault upon peace and a danger to international security. It called upon the North Koreans to cease fire and withdraw north of the 38th parallel.
27 June	: The UN Security Council called upon all members of the UN to support the Republic of Korea; President Truman ordered American air and naval forces to give support.
28 June	: The South Korean Government evacuated Seoul.
29 June	: British and Australian naval forces arrived in Korean waters.
1 July	: The UN decided to create a unified command for Korea; the United States committed ground forces to Korea, and General MacArthur was made Commander in Chief of the UN Command.
2 July	: Australian 77 Squadron flew first combat mission from Japan.
14 July	: The South Korean forces were placed under the UN command.
20 July	: Taejon was taken by the North Koreans.
21 July	: Canadian transport aircraft arrived in Korea.
30 July	: Canadian naval forces arrived in Korean waters; the Naktong River line was established.
1 August	: New Zealand naval units arrived in Korean waters.
28 August	: British 27th Infantry Brigade (Brigadier B. A. Coad) arrived at Pusan.
30 August	: The British government decided to lengthen the period of National Service to two years.
15 September	: UN forces landed at Inchon.
16 September	: UN forces launched an offensive from the Naktong Line.
25 September	: North Korea resistance on the Naktong front failed.
28 September	: Seoul was captured by UN forces; Australian infantry arrived in Korea.
1 October	: South Korean forces advanced north of the 38th parallel.
2 October	: Chou En-lai warned that China would intervene if UN forces entered North Korea.
7 October	: The UN General Assembly authorised UN forces to pursue the North Korean forces into North Korea.
16 October	: The Chinese Peoples Volunteers moved into Korea from Manchuria.
19 October	: Pyongyang, capital of North Korea, fell to UN forces.
26 October	: UN forces reached the Yalu and made contact with Chinese forces; American forces landed in Wonsan.
27 October	: Chinese forces launched their First-phase offensive.
1 November	: Chinese MIG aircraft crossed the Yalu for the first time.
3-18 November	: British 29th Independent Brigade (Brigadier T. Brodie) arrived at Pusan.
7 November	: The 25th Canadian Infantry Brigade began to arrive at Pusan.
20 November	: The 60th Indian Field Ambulance arrived in Korea.
24 November	: General MacArthur launched the drive to the Yalu river.
25 November	: The Chinese Second-phase offensive began.
27 November	: The Chinese offensive penetrated deep into the positions 8th US Army and cut off the 1st Marine Division at Chosin Reservoir.
15 December	: UN forces evacuated Hungnam and Wonsan and formed a line along the 38th parallel.

23 December	General W. H. Walker, Commanding 8th U.S. Army, was killed in a jeep accident. General M. B. Ridgway was appointed to succeed him.
31 December	New Zealand field artillery arrived at Pusan.

1951

4 January	UN forces abandoned Seoul.
25 January	UN forces began Operation Thunderbolt - an advance towards the Han River
1 February	The UN General Assembly condemned China as an aggressor.
21 February	The US 8th Army launched Operation Killer - an advance north.
7 March	The US 8th Army launched Operation Ripper to advance across the Han River.
15 March	UN forces recaptured Seoul.
23 March	Brigadier B. A. Burke succeeded Brigadier B. A. Coad in command of 27th Brigade.
31 March	UN troops reached the 38th parallel.
5 April	UN forces began Operation Rugged to take the Kansas Line.
8 April	Communist forces were cleared from South Korea east of the Imjin by Operation Ripper.
11 April	General MacArthur was relieved of UN Command and succeeded by General Ridgway. General J. A. Van Fleet given command of 8th U.S. Army.
15 April	UN forces formed a defensive line along the 38th parallel.
22 April	Chinese forces began the Fifth-phase offensive. Battle of the Imjin and Battle of the Kapyong.
26 April	Brigadier G. Taylor given Command of 28th Commonwealth Brigade.
30 April	UN forces halted the Chinese offensive on a line to the north of Seoul and the Han River.
16 May	Chinese forces renewed their offensive.
21 May	UN forces counter attacked and pushed the Chinese back north of the 38th parallel.
30 May	UN forces regained the Kansas line.
1 June	US forces commenced Operation Piledriver and advanced towards the Wyoming Line.
13 June	UN forces took Chorwon and Kumwha.
24 June	The Soviet Union proposed talks on a ceasefire.
30 June	The UN command accepted the proposal for armistice talks.
10 July	Armistice talks began at Kaesong.
28 July	The Commonwealth Division was formed under command of General A. J. H. Cassels.
1 August	UN forces began limited offensives to straighten the defensive line.
5 August	Armistice talks were suspended because there were Communist troops in the neutral area.
3-8 October	Commonwealth Division in Operation Commando. Advance to Jamestown Line. Battle of Kowang San and Maryang San.
9 October	Brigadier A. H. G. Ricketts succeeded T. Brodie, 29th Brigade.
25 October	Armistice talks were resumed at Panmunjom.
12 November	UN forces were ordered to confine their operations to active defence.
18 December	The UN Command and Communist forces exchanged lists of POWs.

1952

2 January	:	The UN Command proposed voluntary repatriation of POWs.
12 May	:	General Mark Clark succeeded General Ridgway, UN Command.
28 June	:	Brigadier T. J. Daly (Australia) succeeded Brigadier MacDonald, 29th Brigade.
7 September	:	General M. M. A. R. West succeeded General Cassels, Commonwealth Division.
8 October	:	The UN adjourned Armistice talks due to deadlock on the issue of POWs.
17 November	:	India proposed a compromise solution to the POW issue.
18-19 November	:	Battle of the Hook - Black Watch.
1 December	:	Brigadier D. A. Kendrew succeeded Brigadier Ricketts, 29th Brigade.
3 December	:	The UN General Assembly adopted the Indian compromise solution to the POW issue - no forced repatriation of POWs.

1953

31 January	:	Commonwealth Division went into Corps Reserve.
11 February	:	General M. D. Taylor succeeded General Van Fleet, 8th US Army.
5 March	:	Stalin died.
26 March	:	Brigadier J. G. N. Wilton (Australia) succeeded Brigadier Daly, 28 Commonwealth Brigade.
28 March	:	The UN and Communist forces agreed to exchange sick and wounded prisoners.
8 April	:	Commonwealth Division returned to the line.
20 April	:	Operation 'Little Switch', the exchange of sick and wounded POWs began.
28-29 May	:	Battle of the Hook - Duke of Wellington's Regiment.
8 June	:	The President of South Korea rejected the ceasefire terms.
10 June	:	Communist forces launched an offensive against South Korean positions.
23 June	:	The South Korean Government repeated its objections to the ceasefire terms.
8 July	:	The UN Command and Communists agreed to negotiate an armistice without South Korean participation.
13 July	:	The Chinese forces launched another attack on South Korean positions.
19 July	:	Armistice talks at Panmunjom concluded.
27 July	:	Armistice signed at Panmunjom.
5 August - 6 September	:	Operation 'Big Switch', exchange of POWs took place.

Appendix five

BOOKS WHOLLY OR PARTLY ABOUT BRITISH FORCES

The books are listed in chronological order of first publication in Britain. Most of them are out of print except for those published or reprinted in recent years.

Reginald Thompson. *Cry Korea.* (1951) Reprinted 1974
Correspondent for the Daily Telegraph in Korea until November 1950.

Eric Linklater. *Our Men in Korea.* (1952)
A balanced account of land and sea forces up to July 1951 written for publication by Her Majesty's Stationery Office.

Eric Linklater. *A Year in Space.* (1953)
His account of a tour of the Far East and Pacific, including three chapters about his visit to Commonwealth forces in Korea in July and August 1951.

René Cutforth. *Korean Reporter.* (1952)
Reporter for the BBC in Korea from December 1950 to July 1951.

G. I. Malcolm. *The Argylls in Korea.* (1952)
The Regiment's own story by an officer who served in Korea.

The Royal Ulster Rifles in Korea. (1953)
The Regiment's own story. Author was not named.

John F. A. MacDonald. *The Borderers in Korea.* Date of publication was not given.
The story of the King's Own Scottish Borderers by a Commanding Officer in Korea.

Robert Holles. *Now Thrive The Armourers.* (1952)
Holles was a Sergeant in the Royal Electrical and Mechanical Engineers attached to the Glosters. The story is about a platoon in the Glosters, given fictitious names.

Donald Portway. *Land of the Morning Calm.* (1953)
Colonel Portway was a member of a UN Mission. Chapter 4 touches on British forces.

Julian Tunstall. *I fought in Korea.* (1953)
Tunstall was a soldier in the Middlesex Regiment. He was critical of the UN involvement.

Simon Kent. *A Hill in Korea.* (1953)
A novel about a group of soldiers. In 1956 it was made into a film with the same title. Michael Caine (who served in the Royal Fusiliers in Korea) had his first film part in it.

C. N. Barclay. *The First Commonwealth Division.* (1954)
Brigadier Barclay was given access to Regimental records to write what was in effect a preliminary official history.

R. C. W. Thomas. *The First Commonwealth Division.* (1954)
A general history of the war by Major Thomas.

Anthony Farrar-Hockley. *The Edge of the Sword.* (1954). New Edition, 1985.
The author was Adjutant of the Glosters and captured in the Battle of the Imjin. His experiences in the battle and in captivity,

S. J. Davies. *In Spite of Dungeons.* (1954). Reprinted several times.
Story of captivity by the Padre of the Glosters.

Dennis Lankford. *I Defy.* (1954)
Lieutenant Lankford, Royal Navy, was captured in November 1951. His experiences in captivity.

Derek Kinne. *The Wooden Boxes.* (1955)
Kinne was a soldier in the Royal Northumberland Fusiliers captured in the Battle of the Imjin. His experiences in captivity. See Appendix Two, George Cross.

P. Chambers and A. Landreth (editors). *Called Up. The Personal Experiences of Sixteen National Servicemen Told by Themselves.* (1955)
Two of the stories are about Korea.

A. M. Condron, R. G. Corden, L. V. Sullivan. *Thinking Soldiers.* (Pekin, 1955)
The editors were prisoners of war who decided to stay in Communist China after their release in 1953. Condron, a Royal Marine, later returned to Britain after further thought.

Francis S. Jones. *No Rice For Rebels.* (1956)
A British prisoner of war's story.

D. J. Hollands. *The Dead, The Dying and The Damned.* (1956)
A novel by an officer of the Duke of Wellington's Regiment, based closely on the battalion's service in Korea, including the Battle of the Hook in 1953. Names are fictitious.

M. Tugwell (editor). *The Unquiet Peace. Stories from the Post War Army.* (1957)
Three stories were about Korea - by A. Farrar-Hockley, G. Butler (8 Hussars), and M. Wolff (R. Fusiliers).

Hamish Bain. *The Morning Calm.* (1958)
A novel by a soldier who served in the King's Shropshire Light Infantry. Real name, Hamish Eaton.

Ellery Anderson. *Banner Over Pusan.* (1960)
An oddly named account of the author's part in special operations behind enemy lines.

David Rees. *Korea: Limited War.* (1964)
An excellent history of the war not superseded by any recent work.

Tim Carew. *The Glorious Glosters.* (1970)
A Regimental history including the Korean campaign.

Tim Carew. *Korea: The Commonwealth At War.* (1967). Retitled, *The Korean War.* Pan Books, (1970).
Recounts the exploits of various regiments.

Robert Jackson. *Air War Over Korea.* (1973)
A few mentions of R.A.F. and light aircraft pilots. There are photographs of British aircraft.

B. S. Johnson. *All Bull: The National Servicemen.* (1973)
One personal story is by N. Harman, an officer in the R. Fusiliers.

A. J. Barker. *Fortune Favours The Brave. The Battle of the Hook.* (1974)
Describes the Battles of the Hook in November 1952 (Black Watch) and May 1953 (Duke of Wellington's Regiment. A good impression of soldiering in the static line.

E. D. Harding. *The Imjin Roll.* (1976). Second edition, 1981.
Colonel Harding was a company commander in the Glosters in Korea. The booklet describes the Glosters part in the Battle of the Imjin and prints a full list of men who took part.

Peter Gaston. *The Thirty Eighth Parallel. The British in Korea.* (1976)
Describes the exploits of various regiments. Has a full list of soldiers and Royal Marines killed and medals and honours awarded.

The Die-Hards in Korea. (1976). Second edition, 1983.
The Middlesex Regiment's account of their campaign. The author was not named.

The History of the United Nations Forces in the Korean War. (Seoul 1972-1977)
Six volumes published by the Ministry of National Defence, Republic of Korea.

Ian E. Kaye. *Pick and Shovel Poems.* (1979). (Privately printed)
Several poems relate to the writer's service in the Argylls in Korea.

A. S. McLeod. *Banzai Attack. Korea 1951.* (1981)
A novel about the Argylls in Korea. Author's real name is Alan Barton.

Simon Dunstan. *The Centurion Tank.* (1981) *Armour of the Korean War.* (1982).
Both illustrated books are part of the Osprey Vanguard series.

George Forty. *At War in Korea.* (1982)
Colonel Forty was an officer in the Royal Tank Regiment in Korea. He is now Curator of the Tank Museum, Bovington, Dorset. This is an illustrated history of the land war.

D. J. Sutton (editor). *The Story of the Royal Army Service Corps and Royal Corps of Transport, 1945-1972.* (1983)

David Rees (consultant editor). *The Korean War. History and Tactics.* (1984)
Several military historians have contributed to this illustrated history of the war. One chapter is about the air and sea war.

David Lee. *Eastwards. A History of the Royal Air Force in the Far East 1945-1972.* (1984)

J. Pimlott (editor). *British Military Operations 1945-1984.* (1984)

Robert O'Neill. *Australia in the Korean War. Vol. II. Combat Operations.* (Canberra, 1985).
This official history contains much information about British regiments which served alongside the Australians in 27 and 28 Commonwealth Brigades. Published by the Australian War Memorial and Government Publishing Service.

Peter Thomas. *41 Independent Commando, Royal Marines, Korea 1950-1952.* (1986)
This booklet by Colonel Thomas is a special publication of the RM Historical Society.

Nigel Thomas and Peter Abbott. *The Korean War 1950-53.* (1986)
Osprey Men at Arms series. Illustrates soldiers' battle dress and personal weapons.

Max Hastings. *The Korean War.* (1987)
Covers the ground and air war, but neglects naval operations.

Dan Raschen. *Send Port and Pyjamas!* (1987)
The experiences of a Sapper officer from August 1951 to February 1953.

Appendix six

NOTES ON CONTRIBUTORS

Thomas Ashley Cunningham-Boothe

Born in Manchester, he enlisted in the Lancashire Fusiliers in 1944. In Korea, he served in the Royal Northumberland Fusiliers. After leaving the army in 1953, he lived in Canada for several years. He spent the last ten years of his career in local government administration in Warwickshire, taking early retirement because of severe disabilities resulting from many years of poly-arthritis. He intends to publish a book he has written entitled *How to Live and Work Successfully as a Rheumatoid Arthritic.* He has been very active in the Korean veterans' movement, and first Chairman of the amalgamated B.K.V.A. in 1981-82.

Peter Nelson Farrar

Born in London, he was a National Serviceman in the Royal Fusiliers in Korea. Later he became a schoolteacher and finally a history lecturer at Humberside College of Higher Education. He has retired from teaching but not from research and writing in Korean and other areas of 19th and 20th century History. He hopes that a doctoral study of the statesman Richard Cobden (1804-65) will be published in the near future. He is editor of *The Morning Calm,* the national journal of B.K.V.A. Published twice a year, it includes articles about the war and reviews of books.

Major-General Peter A. Downward CB, DSO, DFC.

Joined the Rifle Brigade in 1942, commissioned in the Prince of Wales' Volunteers (South Lancashire Regiment) and seconded to the Parachute Regiment. Service in North West Europe, India, South East Asia and Eastern Mediterranean. In 1948 he was transferred to the Glider Pilot Regiment. Flew in Berlin airlift in 1948-49. In 1951 he took 1913 Light Liaison Flight to Korea in support of the Commonwealth Division. Awarded DFC in 1952. In 1953, returned to the South Lancashire Regiment and eventually commanded the 1st Battalion in Aden where he was awarded the DSO in 1967. Finally, after other commands, he was appointed Lieutenant Governor (1979-84) of the Royal Hospital, Chelsea. After being Vice-president of B.K.V.A., he became President in 1986. In 1953, he married Hilda Wood of the W.V.S. whom he met in Korea 1952. She died in 1976 and he remarried in 1980, Mrs Mary Proctor.

Colonel Andrew M. Man DSO, OBE.

After holding Staff and other appointments in the Middle East before and during the Second World War, he commanded the 1/7th Bn. The Middlesex Regiment (D.C.O.) in the Normandy invasion and after. Later he commanded the 1st Battalion in Hong Kong and, from August 1950 until March 1951, in Korea. He was awarded the DSO, OBE, French Croix de Guerre, United States Legion of Merit and three times mentioned in Despatches.

Brigadier George Taylor CBE, DSO, KHS.

Commissioned in the West Yorkshire Regiment in 1929. Later, served on staff until 1943 when he was appointed Second in Command of 1st Bn. Worcestershire Regiment. While commanding 5th Bn. Duke of Cornwall's Light Infantry in North West Europe 1944-45, he was twice awarded the DSO. In 1946 he commanded the 2nd Bn. West Yorkshire Regiment in Malaya and then the 1st Battalion in Austria. He commanded 28 Brigade in Hong Kong in 1950 and then in Korea in 1951. In 1952 he was given command of 49 Brigade in Britain, taking it to Kenya for the final campaign 1953-54 against Mau Mau. He is a keen lecturer on military history. The article in this book is an amended version of that which was first published in the *British Army Journal* and also in *Ça Ira* in 1953. He has recently written some memoirs entitled *Infantry Colonel.*

General Sir George Cooper GCB, MC.

Joined the army in 1943. After serving with the Bengal Sappers and Miners, he went to Korea in 1952-53, and was awarded the Military Cross as a Troop Commander in 55 Field Squadron Royal Engineers. Subsequent appointments have included command of 19 Airportable Brigade, South West District, Director of Army Staff Duties and command of South East District. He became Adjutant General and a member of the Army Board in 1981 until retiring in 1984. He is currently Colonel Commandant Royal Engineers and Colonel, The Queen's Gurkha Engineers. His article about the Hook is adapted from the original version published in the *Royal Engineers Journal* (March 1974) under the pseudonym "Nominal".

Anthony P. Eagles

Joined the army in August 1945 and the Gloucestershire Regiment in 1946 - Corps of Drums. With the 1st Battalion in Korea, he was captured in the Battle of the Imjin and spent over two years in P.O.W. camps in North Korea. He was released on 13th August 1953 and left the army in 1954. He has been National Chairman of B.K.V.A. since 1982.

Denis J. Woods

A Regular soldier in the Royal Artillery for five years 1950-55. He volunteered for Korea, serving with 45 Field Regiment 1950-51 and 20 Field Regiment 1952-53. He has held the offices of Secretary of the Cardiff Branch of B.K.V.A., Mid and South Wales Representative on the National Council and Deputy General Secretary of B.K.V.A.

Ron Larby

He was a National Serviceman in the Royal Signals. Volunteered for Korea in 1951 and was attached to 1st Bn. K.S.L.I. He is co-editor of *The Imjin Line,* newsletter of the Herts. and District Branch of B.K.V.A.

Gillian McNair

Gillian McNair, née Hall, joined Q.A.R.A.N.C. as a Nursing Officer in November 1950 aged 23. Served in Britcom General Hospital in Kure, Japan, before going to Seoul. Later in her career, she became Tutor in charge of the School of Nursing at the Royal Victoria Hospital, Netley. She married Lt. Commander Clive McNair R.N.R. in 1961.

Ruth Stone

Joined Q.A.R.N.N.S. as a Nursing Sister. Trained at Bristol Royal Hospital. Commissioned in 1947. Joined H.M.H.S. *Maine* in 1949. She retired in 1976 with the rank of Matron.

Peter Shore

Joined the Royal Navy as a Boy Seaman in 1948, aged 16. Served for 12 years, mostly afloat. As a Navigator's Yeoman and a Clearance Diver, he knew the seas of the world with an unusual intimacy. He now laments the passing of hammocks, runs ashore, oppos and sandy bottoms.

Reuben Holroyd

He was a National Serviceman in the 1st Bn. The Duke of Wellington's Regiment in 1952-54. After demobilization, he established a printing business in Halifax trading as Reuben Holroyd Limited. He prints *The Morning Calm,* the Journal of B.K.V.A. and other periodicals. He is the printer of this book. In the 1960's he privately printed an account of his army experiences under the title *Moving On.*

Other contributors

The editors heartily acknowledge the hard work of successive National Treasurers of B.K.V.A. who helped to make the pre-publication subscription drive a success: Danny Payne who served in 7 R.T.R. in Korea and Ted Simpson who served on H.M.S. *Ceylon.* Also, J. Zammit (H.M.A.S. *Sydney*) of Strathfield, N.S.W., Australia, who promoted interest in the book in Australia and New Zealand and volunteered to collect subscriptions.

Appendix seven

SUBSCRIBERS

With the exception of the first three persons listed, all individual subscribers are listed by their surnames and initials only. In the cases of those who served in more than one unit or ship, the first has been selected.

Field Marshal Sir James Cassels
Major General T. Brodie
Brigadier G. Taylor

8 King's Royal Irish Hussars

Black K. W.
Cudmore R. J.
Currell R.
Dipple E. R.
Erricker R. O.
Huish L. C.
Jones B.
Pearson H.
Peel G.
Rushton D. D.
Sanders R. G.
Southerton R. C. (R.E.M.E.)
Wood R. E.

5 Royal Inniskilling Dragoon Guards

Boardman C.
Bradbury E.
Brindley P. J. (Died 29/1/86)
Dowling T. W.
Hulley J. J.
Jones K. (R.E.M.E.)
Lannen W. T.
Stratford I. T. (R. Signals)
Taylor W.
Whittaker D. (R.E.M.E.)
Williams D. C.
Yeates J.

7 Royal Tank Regiment

Collins H. W.
Mainley R.
Martin-Towsend B.
Payne D. R. (Died 5/8/87)
Rayment C. H.
Ridley L. C.
Vale R. A.
Wright R.

1 Royal Tank Regiment

Cavanagh R.
Clark N. F.
Edwards M.
Elliott C. D. (R.E.M.E.)
Petch E. B.
Poole V. D.
Pountain R. D.

Royal Artillery

Barlow R. T. (Died 5/2/87)
Emberson A. W. J.
Pike W. G. H.
Singleton R. J. B.
Warhurst R. G.

45 Field Regiment R. A.

Atkins S. F. (R.E.M.E.)
Bailey C.
Bamford C. J.
Barnett R. T.
Beckingham E. H.
Caley W. R.
Davies C. B.
Fieldson T.
Gould E. A. B.
Hailes G.
Harbison J. W. E.
Knight E. G.
Matthews A. A.
Maytum P. W.
Moody A.
Morton S. E.
Norris R.
Rees E. G.
Ryder C. G. N.
Seymour E. J.
Smith A.
Stevens R. A. (R.E.M.E.)
Stone K. R.
Stowe E. S.
Thompson L.
Wells F. H.
Westrope P.
Woodhead E.
Woods D. J.

14 Field Regiment R. A.

Black F. D.
Callaghan C.
Clowsley P. A.
Commander G. W.
Fry P. B.
Saundercock V. G.
Williams I.

20 Field Regiment R. A.

Bridge K.
Kitching J.
Livingstone J. A.
Prince C. W.
Sargeant E. C.
Shutt W. A.
Stephenson P. B.
Stevens R. F.

170 Independent Mortar Battery

Bell G.
Cole W. C.
Dunnachie M. E.
Fowle M. C.
Hurst G. C.
Kitchener O. R.

120 Mortar Battery R. A.

Bunce G. T.
Carter A.
Fletcher K. G.

61 Light Regiment R.A.

Bartlett E. P. (R.E.M.E.)
MacFarlane A. M.
Marriott F. C.
Parr M. T.
Sussman N.
Temple A. D. (R.E.M.E.)

42 Mortar Battery, 61 Light Regiment R. A.

Barton R.
Collings T. J.
Ferguson A. Mc C.
Ferrari B. D.
White M.

15 Locating Battery, 61 Light Regiment R. A.

Alldritt R. J.
Carroll G. J.
Flynn B.
Fox R. R.
Forrow L. D.
Turner H. E.

74 Medium Battery

Young J. A.

Argyll and Sutherland Highlanders

Bogart C. G.
Kaye I. E.
Mailer-Howat G. M. M.
Peters E.
Ross P. I. M.
Searle R. E.
Stone R.
Walford J. E.

Black Watch

Barnes A. D.
Cameron G. R.
Cross K.
Crowter R.
Green N.
Jackson G.
Munn P. J.
Rennie C.
Stuart W.

The Duke of Wellington's Regiment

Bailes J. S.
Bangs P. J.
Billings G. O.
Dickie T. T.
Ellison D.
Fetch K.
Holroyd R.
Keld K.
Morgan E. J.
Oliver B. R.
Sargeant J. E.
Simpson M.
Taylor R.
Wilson-Leary G. H.
Wood D. J.

Durham Light Infantry

Bridgewater I. S.
Collinson W. F.
Dyke P. A.
Hayton R. H.
Hedges W. R.
Lown K. R.
Maggs E. A.
Morgan O. B.
Murton P. A.
Owers A. R.
Parker D.
Scott J. W.
Stockton E.

Gloucestershire Regiment

Adams W. L.
Adlem A. R.
Allott G.
Birt E. J.
Bostock F. W. D.
Carter F. E.
Collins J. W. C.
Curness L. S.
Davis R. L. J.
Dimmelow B.
Eagles A. P.
Hall A. J.
Green G. E.
Hawkins B.
Howard J. F. N. (A.C.C.)
Jarman R.
Leveridge H. F.
Madgwick E. C.
Mercer S.
Morris J. T.
Newhouse G. E.
Panting R. E. G.
Parfit A. R.
Roberts G. F.
Smith K. F.
Strong F. G. (A.P.T.C.)
Thompson G. M. (R.E.M.E.)
Towsend K. L.
Vanburg P. T. E.
Walker J. M.
Webb S. E.
Wells F. J.
Wells R. T.
Wingham L. E.
Wood J. W.
Worthington B. (R.E.M.E.)

Middlesex Regiment

Banner G.
Bosworth P. R.
Boydell S. (R.A.M.C.)
Cooper A. G. W.
Edwards A. R. F.
Fitch R. F.
Gilbertson R. H.
Guarnieri J. H.
Man A. M.
Mound V. H.
Parnell W. E.
Paternoster R. S.
Smith R. T.
Spicer H. E.
Strevett G. T.
Waldron A. E. F.
Ward L. J. H.

King's Own Scottish Borderers

Chandler J. H.
Coleman C. A.
Grundy J. R. (A.C.C.)
Hill R.
Huson R. A.
McCurdy M. M.
Ormston J. T.

King's Regiment

Peers R. N. R.
Trigg N. F.
Wasley C. P.

King's Shropshire Light Infantry

Bale A. R.
Bianchi J. G.
Chakley A.
Crewe J. W. D.
Eaton G. D.
Eaton H. B.
Edwards J. A.
Fellows A.
Pickersgill L. W.
Ford A.
Frankland G. J.
Goldberg D. R.
Harvey F. E.
Hick P. M.
Hird T. A.
Kamsler W. P.
Lees J. K.
Middle G. H.
Murphy J. E.
Oliver H. J.
Peake G.
Peate E. E.
Sankey E. E.
Sherwood S. R.
Steel G.
Webb E.
Williams D. A.
Wright H.

Royal Fusiliers (City of London Regiment)

Baldwin C. J.
Bird R. E.
Brown S. F.
Farrar P. N.
Gardner J. F.
Gorton G. (R.A.M.C.)
Harrison F. R.
Hawkes B. E.
Hill D. J.
Hills M.
Houslop F. W.
Lockmuller L.
Mitchell W. C.
Payne L. A.
Randall D. E.
Rouse A. H.
Rushbrook R. W.
Russel G.
Smith B.
Snelling D. R.
Walsh A. E.

Royal Leicestershire Regiment

Airey M.
Barry J. F. (R.A.M.C.)
Cleaver P. J.
Cox R. W.
Fletcher W. J.
Green D. W.
Green K.
Hare J. A. E.
Hiom D. A.
Jubb D. A.
Kemp L. J.
Leighton F.
Pugh A. G.
Shorter F.
Small J. M.
Stansbie R. W.
Worrall C.

Royal Norfolk Regiment

Barham J.
Buller W. V.
Chapman W. C.
Cook G. A.
Critcher R. S.
Daws G. A.
Dixon P.
Hanwell P. J.
Hart S. W.
Lloyd W. T.
Minards H. G.
Nutter K. E.
Powlesland A. C.
Pownall R. S.
Price F. J.
Rintoul I.
Smith D. T.
Wicker P.

Royal Northumberland Fusiliers

Buckley H. H.
Barrett T. W.
Beasley L. (Died 12/6/86)
Coates H.
Cragg D. W.
Cumberford J.
Cunningham-Boothe T. A.
Johnson J. R.
Kinne D. G.
Leith-MacGregor R.
McFall T.
Matthews D.
Preece S. E.
Prout D. H.
Richards N. J.
Rowse P. J.
Rushworth N.
Stephenson D.
Stones G.
Strachan D. E.
Thompson T.

Royal Ulster Rifles

Axford A.
Charley W. R. H.
Clancy S. P.
Dawson J. T.
Doyle M. R.
Farrell J. W.
Foster E. J.
Johnson F. R. C.
Jones L.
Kennedy N.
Lowry S.
McHaffey T. B.
Moore T. A.
Noble W. J. D.
O'Kane H.
Revill R.
Roberts R. F.
Scully P. M. P.
Smith F. R. (A.C.C.)
Winter S. E.

The Welch Regiment

Davies W. H.
Flynn T. J.
Jones A.
Lee E. R.
McLean J. R.
Rees D. J. L.
Roberts C. N.
Walsh J. P. (R.E.M.E)
Williams W.
Winstanley W. J.

The Royal Scots

McQueen J.
Sommerville D. P.

H.Q. Attachments

Christie G. (Highland Light Infantry)
Marshall W. H. (Royal Scots Fusiliers)

North Staffordshire Regiment

Lear J.
Lowe W. H.

Queen's Own Cameron Highlanders

Morrison B.
Wilson W. A.

Royal Warwickshire Regiment

Adcock G.
Goodman D.
Russell A.

Royal Engineers

Bartholomew J. L. W.
Beddoes J. H.
Cope D. F.
Cormack J. N.
Crotch R. E.
Diamond G. B.
Fairway E.
Fletcher G.
Griffiths D. S.
Haighton D. A.
Harding G. L.
Hazzard C. C.
Hills D. L.
Holloway E. E.
Leslie P.
McKay A. J. R.
Murfitt P. J.
Myers E. C. W.
Oatway R. V.
Palmer L. N.
Pickard J. J.
Raschen D. G.
Robertson T. W.
Stone G. F.
Sharp E. J.
Wilby G.
Younger A. E.

Royal Signals

Boxall R. K.
Briggs R. N.
Coford A. W.
Comley A. A.
Cope J. A.
Drummond P.
Fuller J. B.
Goode T. F.
Johnson H.
Larby R.
Lawson J. W.
Lofty P. A.
Micklefield J.
Pearson L.
Simpson E. J.

Royal Army Service Corps

Andrews J. R.
Biggin B. A.
Clarke D. E.
Colquhoun J.
Ellis E.
Elphick V.
Evans G.
Hall F.Melville P. S.
Hallows A. W.
Howarth J.
Hurdley A. E.
Keep R. J.
Long C. N.
Lucas A. W.
McDermott C.
Moulsdale R.
Pye M. A.
Riggals J. S.
Robinson P. E.
Sawdon D.
Townsend N. F.
Winning W.

Royal Army Medical Corps

Davies T. I.
Delahaye E.
Rosser E. M.

Royal Electrical and Mechanical Engineers

Beevor E. D.
Bradley A. H.
Connell J.
Crewe G. D.
Dagg R. J.
Dale S.
Dodd G. A.
Hart J. H.
Hooper A. W.
Humphreys C. B. G.
Jeffes H. R.
Miles R. G.
Nickerson J.
Pearson G.
Porter B. H. W.
Rawlings P. W. R.
Simpson D. C.
Snow M. C.

Royal Army Ordnance Corps

Aggett P. R.
Charlton T. L.
Davies G. M.
Harris A.
Pulcella M. R.
Thompson O. J.

Royal Military Police

Bearwood W. J.
Chase J.
Elmes J. R.
Lea S. M.
Moffat A. N.
Moody A. J.
Smith J.
Stead G. S. P.

Army Catering Corps

Wise N.

Royal Army Pay Corps

Davies P. C.
Mansfield R. A.

Royal Army Educational Corps

West P. J.

Queen Alexandra's Royal Army Nursing Corps

Akroyd P. M. (Based in U.K.)
Britton M. R. (Based in U.K.)
McNair E. J.

1903 Air Observation Post Flight

Addington D. F. C.
Dodd R. I.

1913 Light Liaison Flight

Downward P. A.
King T. W.

Royal Army Chaplains Department

Davies S. J.
McKinnon M. C.
Preston F. A.
Tyler H. G.

Norwegian Mobile Army Surgical Hospital

Pederson L. U. Chaplain

3 Royal Australian Regiment

Allan M. J.
Bickle R. H.
Hammond R. E.
Horgan B. G.
Keys A. G. W.
Kirkland F.
Knowles P. J.
Matsen W. S.
Thompson J. J.
Warhurst R. A.
Forrester W. G.

1 R.A.R.

Beater R. E. (Died)
Blade B. C.
Bowd P.
Douglass W. F.

R. A. Signals

Moore J.

77 Squadron R.A.A.F.

Potts H. C.

Britcom Broadcasting Unit

O'Brien G. D.

Canadian Army

Bougie C. R.
Rank J. K.

Royal Canadian Regiment

Scott G

Royal Canadian Artillery

McLean F. E.

Luxembourg Platoon

Faber R.

United States Army

Coe W. C.
Woodruff W. D.

Royal Marines

Cox C.
Curd E. J.
Groom A. F.
Richards G. R.
Thorpe W. D.
Wagg R. K.

H.M.S. Alacrity

Spurrier J. C. W.

H.M.S. Belfast

Harvey L. J.

H.M.S. Birmingham

Ingram P. F.

H.M.S. Black Swan

Williams D. J.

H.M.S. Cardigan Bay

Beach D. C.
Emery H. J.
Hague J. L.

H.M.S Ceylon

Ayling R. E.
Excell K. H.
Harding E. R.
Packham R. L.
Randall T. H.
Savage J. F.
Seymour G. W.
Simpson E. M.
Whyte E.

H.M.S. Charity

Dick R. C.
Griffin D. A.

H.M.S. Cockade

Darwood D. R.
Harris E. H.
Wilson R. J.

H.M.S. Comus

Billingham B. R.
Kane R. B.
Rand F. D.

H.M.S. Concord

Brown P. C.
Freemantle J. T.
Lees F.

H.M.S. Consort

Gray W. L.

H.M.S. Constance

Balderson E. W.
Prior H.
Thorne W. F. D.

H.M.S. Cossack

Cain P. J.
Price J. F.
Quartermaine A.
Relf P. R.

H.M.S. Crane

Hughes J. M.

H.M.S. Glory

Ashdown K. W.
Burton S. A. J.
Cook P. W.
Grant L.
Neep R.
Oliver A. J.
Parkes D. R. B.
Parkes T. A. J.

H.M.S. Kenya

Robertson J. W.

H.M.S. Modeste

Cox K. H.

H.M.S. Morecambe Bay

Moyle-Keen F.

H.M.S. Ocean

Fordham J. D. S. (807 Sqdn)
Froud J. R. (807 Sqdn)

H.M.S. Opossum

Shore R. P.
Wood M. J.

H.M.S. Theseus

Fisher D. (807 Sqdn)
Milner C. K.
Payne T.
Renwick P. H.

H.M.S. Triumph

Green J. A.
Nunn D. R.

H.M.S. Unicorn

Hammett J. L.
Kelleway R. F.

H.M.S Whitesand Bay

Drake R. M.
Woodham P. J.

H.M. Hospital Ship Maine

Stone R. (Q.A.R.N.N.S.)
Wood M. E. (Q.A.R.N.N.S.)

Danish Hospital Ship Jutlandia

Hill Rigmor D. (Danish Nursing Council)

H.M.N.Z.S. Tutira

Moss D. J.

H.M.A.S. Bataan

Bateman F. J.
David G. C.
Sexton R. J.
Smyth D. H. D.
Webber C. J.

H.M.A.S. Condamine

Fazio V. B.

H.M.A.S. Sydney

Barlow B. H.
Gorringe J. F.
Gullick N. C.
Langrell J. B.
Lascelles R. S.
Lelievre P. M.
MacGregor M. M.
Wilson F. E.
Zammit A. J.
Zammit D. J.
Zammit S. V.

H.M.A.S. Tobruk

Adlam H. C.

H.M.A.S. Warramunga

Evans R. E.

Royal Australian Navy

Brown R. L.
Diver R.
Given S. F.
Hinchliffe L. M.
Jeppesen J. C.
Sampson W. G. T.
Simpson S. R.
Torrington R. J.

The Sir Jules Thorn Charitable Trust
West Midlands Regional Committee B.K.V.A.
B.K.V.A. Branches: Warwickshire, Greater Manchester, Preston and District, Ipswich and District, Wirral and West Cheshire, West Wales, Kent Invicta, Stoke and District, Northumbria, Bedfordshire, Shropshire, Birmingham, Sussex, Hertfordshire and District, York.

Royal Tank Regiment Association
Duke of Wellington's Regiment
R.A.S.C./R.C.T. Association
Welch Regiment Museum
Royal Regiment of Wales Association
K.S.L.I. Museum
Queen's Royal Irish Hussars
Royal Ulster Rifles Association
Royal Irish Rangers
Essex Regiment Association
Royal Artillery Association
B.L.E.S.M.A.
Returned Services League of Australia
H.M.A.S. Hobart Association
Imperial War Museum
National Army Museum
Foreign and Commonwealth Office Library
Warwick District Council
Warwick District N.A.L.G.O. Branch
British Embassy, Republic of Korea

Bull A. G.
Burke C.
Catchpole B. A.
Clark J. C.
Charlick R. G.
Dudley F.
Foster P.
Gaines A. B.
Godfree A. F. P.
Grant W.
Greenway E. M.
Hardy D. W.
Hardy P. R.
Hardy R. A.
Hardy R.
Hardy S.
Hardy T. A.
Head M. A.
Hoare J. E.
King J.
Laurie J. A.
Marvelly J. K. R.
Miley A. H.
Morris B. L.
O'Neill R.
Palmer D.
Partridge B. M.
Playford G. R.
Sinnott E. M.
Smith O. F.
Stephenson G. R.
Winch G. D.